This book is dedicated to sustainability professionals around the world who have demonstrated that you can do well by doing good. The late Ray Anderson lived by this motto and we have him to thank for his leadership. Many others have touched me along this journey, including Amory Lovins, who continues to show us that business can lead the world in making a profit while also making the world a better place for us all. Thank you to those who have been brave enough to show us the way and for the believers who support them.

Mainstreaming Corporate Sustainability

Using Proven Tools to Promote Business Success

Suzanne Farver

Published by:

GreenFix, LLC
PO Box 420
Cotati, CA 94931
www.mainstreamingsustainability.com

ISBN: 1484135326
ISBN-13: 978-1484135327

Cover Design: Natalie Zanecchia
Back Cover Photo: Pat Sudmeier

First printed in 2013

Printed in the USA

CONTENTS

Acknowledgements

This book is the culmination of the efforts of many years of preparation, and without the help and support of my family and friends, it would not have come to fruition. I have had many mentors along the way, but there are a few who have stood out and have supported this work in particular.

Thank you to Dr. Annie Brown, who blazed her own trail in publishing and with whom I have shared many hikes and conversations in the mountains of Colorado. To the brilliant Anna Deavere Smith, thank you for your encouragement and confidence. Thank you to Clint Van Zee for his love and support, and for the many words of wisdom and encouragement along the way. Thanks as well to Emily Celano, whose research and editing expertise helped to delineate important resources for me, as well as to Dr. Jack Spengler and Dr. Ramon Sanchez at Harvard University for their support of Emily's work. Associate Dean Mary Higgins gave me the help I needed when I was just beginning this venture, and I am grateful for her guidance and support. Christine Wilikinson provided essential legal advice. Natalie Zanecchia was instrumental in cover design and in bringing a unified look to the figures and tables throughout.

Finally, I would like to thank Dr. Matthew Gardner, my team teacher for our class at Harvard University Extension School. Matt is a talented speaker and instructor and is passionate about the field. He possesses a wealth of experience guiding businesses that are facing the challenges of mainstreaming sustainability into their operations.

To all of you on this journey, thank you for your friendship and camaraderie. We have an enormous responsibility to care for this earth and to leave it a better place for our children's children and beyond. Namaste.

Preface

A large body of work about corporate sustainability is available today in the form of white papers published by leading nonprofit groups, comprehensive handbooks with step-by-step forms and templates, and international standards customized to various industries. There are terrific company profiles as well as biographies of business leaders, which explain the triumphs and challenges of taking on the kinds of changes needed to move a company toward a more sustainable and responsible position.

The purpose of this book is to provide a solid overview of the resources that are available to today's business leaders. Who are some of the leading voices in this field? What tools have they used and what do they have to offer? What are some of the toughest challenges? How do you begin this journey for your own company? How do you avoid being overwhelmed by the volume of material offered on the subject?

Each chapter provides a basic overview of the fundamental areas involved in guiding a corporation toward a more sustainable future. Although there are still many new ideas and approaches being developed, the basic topics have become well established in the field of sustainability. Seeing how these principles have been applied in the industry can help you to see how they can be used for your own company or organization. The end of each chapter includes suggestions for further reading to help you dig more deeply into particular areas of interest.

By the time you finish this book, you will have a solid understanding of what sustainability means for today's modern global institutions and what tools might be most appropriate for your organization. You will have a grasp of the organizations leading the charge for businesses and governments around the world as well as the kinds of concepts they have developed to meet the challenges of managing resources responsibly while enriching society.

The inspiration for writing this book began when I was asked to develop a new course called Corporate Sustainability Strategy at Harvard University Extension School. The course has been offered with weekly introductory essays along with supplementary reading materials. I felt that the students would benefit from having a book that served the same purpose—an overview plus a set of expanded references compiled into one text. Published a chapter at a time in 2012 on the course website, it is now offered here to our students as well as those interested in pursuing a comprehensive sustainability system for their organization.

More information on the class, along with other classes in the Environmental and Sustainability graduate studies program at Harvard University Extension School, can be found at the following website: http://www.extension.harvard.edu/.

Note about reference style: Students in the graduate program at Harvard are required to use the American Psychological Association (APA) style for reference citations in their papers and for their masters thesis or capstone presentations. As this style is also required in the Corporate Sustainability Strategy class, the book has been written using this style for references.

List of Figures

List of Tables

Chapter 1

Introduction to Sustainability

Where sustainability works best is where an organization's leadership gets it and wants it to happen and enables it to happen so everyone from the person who sweeps the floor to the finance director feels part of that conversation.
— Will Day, Chairman, Sustainable Development Commission

What is Sustainability?

The word *sustainability* seems to have many different meanings floating about these days. Politicians use it when talking about keeping the government from running into debt. Environmentalists think of sustainability from the perspective of maintaining resources and reducing pollution. Farmers think about having enough water and fertile soil to grow healthy crops. Everyday folks think about sustainability from the standpoint of paying the bills and keeping food on the table. But what does it mean to use this term in relation to a modern corporation?

Many of you are probably familiar with the Bruntland Commission's definition of sustainable development (Bärlund, 2004-05):

> Development that meets the needs of current generations without compromising the ability of future generations to meet their own needs

This is an excellent and well-accepted definition for the purposes of making sustainable development and policy decisions. However, for a corporation, it helps to have a bit more flesh to dig into. What about the human resources side of sustainability? Shouldn't sustainability include that as well?

In addition, how can a corporation identify a planning timeline? How far into the future should it plan? Are we talking about the needs of current generations within the control of the corporation, or does it include its entire supply chain and future generations as well? What about the demands of customers or suppliers who may have different priorities? What if the increase in price of certain resources is forcing a corporation to choose products that have a negative effect on society or the environment? How do you make the right choices?

Mainstreaming Sustainability

To answer these questions, we need to understand how to drive sustainability into the fabric of the organization such that it becomes systemic. Every system within the organization must include parameters to encourage better decision making regarding not just economic concerns but also environmental and social concerns. This is what *mainstreaming* sustainability means—making sustainability part of a company's DNA.

The tools and concepts included in this book can be used to help guide a corporation along the path toward mainstreaming sustainability. This includes setting the initial vision; engaging with various stakeholders to understand their concerns and to develop a strategy; communicating with suppliers, governing bodies, or nongovernmental organizations (NGOs) to ensure full collaboration; complying with rules and regulations while striving to perform beyond those requirements; and measuring performance along the way to ensure that policies and decisions are supported and revised if necessary for optimum performance.

The goal of sustainability is exactly that: a goal. It may never be fully achieved, and even when a company is close to achieving that goal, it may only be for a short time. The late Ray Anderson of Interface coined the phrase "striving for Mount Sustainability." Sometimes it feels like a long climb to the top, with narrow curves and boulders along the way. Tension will always exist between the three areas of responsibility—environmental, economic, and social—that may be difficult to completely satisfy all the time for everyone. But striving for that balance is key. It is that tension that keeps every person in the organization on his or her toes, looking for the best solution to every challenge. As the quote from Will Day at the beginning of this chapter emphasizes, sustainability leadership needs to come from the top, but it also requires buy-in from everyone in the organization.

Corporate Sustainability Defined

Most sustainability experts today argue that corporate sustainability involves three basic resource areas that are impacted by any company: environmental, social, and economic. Some refer to these as "the three responsibilities" or "the triple bottom line." The responsibilities of a company within these three areas can be described in various ways, but well-accepted terms include environmental responsibility, social well-being, and economic prosperity. These encompass the spectrum of what is involved for a company doing business in today's global marketplace. For any corporation, the day-to-day challenge is making its sustainability goals *operational*. Does the Bruntland definition of sustainability provide enough guidance to do so?

This brings us back to our initial series of questions. How do you define sustainability such that it drives the operational decisions that are made on a daily basis? Defining sustainability in a way that encourages transparency and accountability is also important. This makes everyone in the company responsible for the advancement of sustainability goals. Collective responsibility and accountability drives quality and reduces waste.

For these reasons, the following definition is proposed for corporate sustainability:

> Corporate sustainability means balancing environmental stewardship, social well-being, and economic prosperity while driving toward a goal of long-term success for the health of the company and its stakeholders. A sustainable corporation is transparent in its management of these responsibilities and is held accountable to its stakeholders for its results.

This definition implies that the balancing effort is a constant challenge for the organization. Figure 1.1 below illustrates the tension between these three responsibilities with the sustainability "sweet spot" in the middle.

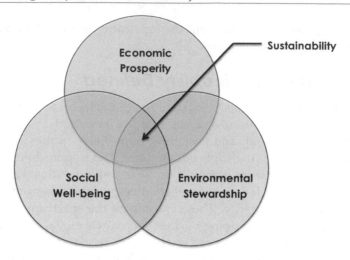

Figure 1.1: Sustainability "Sweet Spot"

Managing these responsibilities means always striving to strike the right equilibrium between all three, while also being accountable to the stakeholders who are concerned about any one or all of those responsibilities. Answering to the stakeholders' concerns is an important part of any company especially in today's age of hyper-communication.

Transparency is also required, meaning that an organization must communicate openly and honestly regarding the risks it faces as a company as well as its plans for improvement. Some companies see this as a threat, but woe to those who fail to disclose information that is later revealed in a negative light. Such an incident can foster distrust and may cause a company's reputation to falter.

The three areas of responsibility will be covered in detail in separate chapters. Sustainability reporting and accountability will be analyzed as well, including the various tools and concepts that companies can employ to help make objective decisions with stakeholder help regarding what and how to report progress and challenges.

Thinking ahead constitutes a large part of the planning process for sustainability. Planning for success as well as possible breakdowns reflect sound management principles of any management system. Using fewer resources, designing a positive and supportive workplace, and paying attention to important stakeholder concerns create a more productive and a more profitable company. Mainstreaming sustainability throughout a company is simply good business.

A Positive View

The idea of approaching sustainability from a positive perspective or framework is one that is emphasized by many in the field. Pollution prevention or P2 is one example of such an approach. Its basic premise is to improve business processes overall in order to increase efficiency thereby reducing the overall amount of toxic emissions. This is promoted by the Environmental Protection Agency (EPA) as a positive solution to pollution, as opposed to charging fees and requiring permits for toxic waste.

Other examples of employing a positive approach include the ideas promoted by Amory Lovins and the Rocky Mountain Institute (RMI), which, for over thirty years, has consistently encouraged business-led solutions to the world's most challenging energy problems. With a mission to drive the efficient and restorative use of the world's resources, RMI is recognized as a leader at creating positive solutions while working with a variety of unexpected partners, including Walmart and the Pentagon.

Another example of a positive vision for sustainability is the Appreciative Inquiry model, an approach to developing organizations centered on finding constructive resolutions and solutions by identifying the common positive values among its participants. Appreciative Inquiry was originally developed by David Cooperrider in 2005 and it has since become popular among many sustainability professionals.

Numerous permutations of positive thinking have been promoted throughout modern society, from Norman Vincent Peale's *The Power of Positive Thinking* to the plethora of books on success available in today's market. Whatever the package, the idea is sound and an effort will be made to emphasize positive solutions throughout this book.

By harnessing the collective consciousness of an organization in a positive manner, people can be inspired to new heights. Creativity can be unleashed with more energy to work together in a more holistic manner. Many psychological studies support the connection between happiness and better health or longevity. People are also more productive in a workplace that supports a positive vision for change rather than a negative environment of threats. Research has shown that people stay at their jobs for reasons other than just a paycheck. Work approval and support often trump salary on the list of reasons for remaining in a particular work environment.

Part of creating a Sustainability Management System (SMS) includes monitoring results and promoting continuous improvement. This is another example of employing a positive vision at work. Companies must strive to improve their processes every time they undergo review. Rather than fixating on a problem, focusing on *improvement* helps to keep the emphasis on positives. Emphasis on positives not only improves the process itself; it also improves morale. While some are obsessed with problems and mistakes., turning that negative energy around to focus on a positive vision and continual improvement helps to keep everyone motivated and happy.

Emphasizing What Works

To incorporate sustainability into an organization therefore requires that we look for what works in an organization. Emphasizing those positives enables the company to act responsibly in the three areas of sustainability. The tangible results of this responsible behavior may be a series of statements describing the organization's positive view. As examples, such statements might reflect core values like honesty, integrity, respect, or fairness. Because these terms resonate with most people as commonly held values, their use reinforces positive and constructive behavior.

If an organization creates an internal assessment program within the SMS, documentation of sustainability successes creates a synergistic drive. This drive gains momentum within the organization and will eventually become self-supporting. Employees are encouraged to participate and offer new ideas as management review provides rewards and support. Pride in accomplishments permeates the organization. Success therefore becomes an everyday means of doing business.

This positive energy and excitement is what supports sustainability over the long term. There should be no end to the continuous improvement process. Successes are built on real experiences in the organization. Reporting on those successes becomes a priority in itself, supporting further improvement and innovation.

Responsibility from the ISO Perspective

What does responsibility mean from a corporate or business standpoint? How do you frame this idea such that it can be managed and made operational within the organization?

The International Organization for Standardization (ISO) can help us here. Founded in 1947, ISO is a nongovernmental, independent organization made up of representatives from various national standards organizations in over 160 countries and coordinated in Geneva, Switzerland. Since its inception, ISO has developed over nineteen thousand individual standards to guide the operation of business and technology around the world. ISO has established industry-specific standards as well as general standards emphasizing environmental, social, and quality factors. Some of you may be familiar with ISO 14001, which governs environmental responsibility.

ISO standards are identified by numbers, which helps them to cross language barriers, but for those of us studying the standards, the numbers can be confusing. Throughout this book, an effort will be made to link each standard's title with its area of focus to help avoid confusion.

ISO 26000, which addresses social responsibility, provides an excellent framework for understanding the idea of responsibility from an organizational standpoint. It stresses the importance of directly incorporating environmental, social, and economic concerns in decision-making processes. It also emphasizes the importance of holding an organization accountable for any decisions made in this regard. Such accountability necessarily implies being transparent in all communication, behaving ethically, and accounting for the various interests of the organization's stakeholders. Compliance with laws and regulations is, of course, required, as is consideration of international norms and cultural concerns (ISO, 2009).

An organization must understand society's expectations as well as the environment's carrying capacity. This goes beyond the legal requirements, extending to shared societal values and expectations. It also demands a proactive stance, which relates back to the notion of positive values—in essence, improving processes and activities to avoid triggering regulatory requirements and avoiding the need to be in compliance as the activities are *beyond compliance*.

For a company operating on a multinational scale, expectations for responsibility may vary widely. They may diverge according to a particular country or culture. They may also differ in accordance with the particular industry in which the organization operates. In this case, international norms can be helpful in determining the best guidelines. One such example is the Universal Declaration of Human Rights (United Nations, 1948).

Integrating Responsibilities

It is the day-to-day business of an organization that impacts society, the environment, and the economic prosperity of those involved with the company. Therefore, the idea of responsibility should form an integral part of company management. Likewise, accountability should be emphasized at all levels of the company. Responsibility and accountability should constitute what every employee does every day. Every decision should reflect these goals and the implementation thereof should be carefully reviewed and recorded to reflect the impacts of all business activities.

Relationships with other organizations or businesses can also have a significant impact. Therefore, it may be necessary for businesses and NGOs to work together to properly address their responsibilities. This can even include working with competitors (possibly through trade organizations), suppliers, customers, or other stakeholders (ISO, 2009).

Managing Responsibilities

The various ISO standards provide a framework for managing the three areas of responsibility. They can be combined to form a customized management system to drive not only responsibility for environmental and social concerns but also quality and improved business performance. The ISO 9001 Quality Management System can be supplemented with a number of ISO and other management system standards. Some such standards can be certified by an outside auditor; others are merely suggested guidelines. In later chapters, these standards will be discussed in greater detail.

The following presents a list of the most commonly used management system standards:

- ISO 14001: *Environmental Management Systems*
- ISO 26000: *Guidance on Social Responsibility*
- ISO 50001: *Energy Management Systems*
- ISO 31000: *Risk Management*
- Occupational Health and Safety Standard (OHSAS) 18001: *Occupational Health and Safety Management Systems*
- Publicly Available Specification (PAS) 2050: *Specification for the Assessment of the Life Cycle Greenhouse Gas Emissions of Goods and Services*
- Australian Standard (AS) 8000: *Good Governance Principles*
- AS 8002: *Organizational Codes of Conduct*
- BS 8900: *Guidance for Managing Sustainable Development*

Using these standards to create a customized management system is a robust way to incorporate sustainability into a company or organization—whether that company is large or small. The management system therefore becomes integrated into the processes of the company, *mainstreaming* the policies and systems into the fabric of the organization itself.

Use of a standards-based system is more effective than using a step-by-step process as promoted by some sustainability guides. Taking a few steps toward sustainability may seem tempting and may sound like a potentially successful approach, but simply starting an initiative or two through a step-by-step process can lead to failure. In contrast, integrating these standards into the management systems of the company can ensure a much higher rate of success and can also promote continued and future value for the company.

A Few Testimonials

Why go through all this trouble? Employment of a management system brings a much higher propensity for ultimate success. As we'll discuss in Chapter 3, companies who take sustainability seriously tend to do better in their field. However, the case is still building for this idea. Many CEOs give it only lip service; others who realize its true value have found real benefits from its pursuit.

Below are a few quotes from various experts in the field. The following quote from Xerox expresses the systemic requirement of sustainability (Environmental Leader, 2012, p. 43):

> *At Xerox, we continue to believe that for sustainability to be meaningful, it must be incorporated into an organization's business operations. Sustainability initiatives separate and apart from your fundamental business operations are meaningless.*
>
> —*Wendi Latko, Xerox*

The following quote from a sustainability consultant describes the need for a thorough and complete commitment throughout a company, including input from the company's stakeholders (Environmental Leader, 2012, pp. 42-43):

> *I have consulted for several companies in print and paper over the last few years, training and preparing them for sustainable development programs on the basis that their markets have taken those directions.*
>
> *In all cases but one, the companies have gone halfway and will not finish the job.*
>
> *Halfway means management approaching sustainability with great enthusiasm and forming committees to implement the strategy, made public their intentions [mostly too soon] and then, as they fail to persuade their sales people to move the strategy into the markets [through ignorance at both buyer and seller levels], given up the program.*
>
> *Only one has recognized the need to develop internal sustainably based structures, external supplier sustainability-based procurement criteria, and external market research to place the program in the right hands, before taking the program public and staying the course.*
>
> *This is not "quick fix" business technology. It is changing the ways companies operate from start to finish and it takes time.*
>
> —*Derek Smith, Derek Smith & Associates, LLC*

And this from a prominent auditing firm regarding the trend of sustainability (Environmental Leader, 2011, p. 30):

The recent acquisition of sustainability consulting firms by Deloitte Touche illustrates the fact that corporate responsibility, including sustainability reporting and carbon management, will become business as usual in the near future.

—*Dontien S. Ingram-Moore*

Secret Sauce: Performance Frameworks

In addition to the commitment of management and staff, and with the guidance of an SMS, the "secret sauce" for true success in any business pursuing sustainability can be the use of a performance framework. Not many are familiar with such an idea, but performance frameworks push a company to keep track of "leading indicators" that truly drive performance. Future chapters will discuss this concept in more detail, but for now, think of performance frameworks as providing a sneak peek into the future. They provide a way of keeping track of where a company is going rather than where it has been.

Performance frameworks provide the structure necessary to encourage productivity, effective management, and quality improvement. Various performance frameworks exist around the world, but one that is recognized and respected in the United States is the Baldrige Criteria for Performance Excellence. Those who participate in the program may be eligible to receive a related award, but any company can follow the criteria and achieve the results with or without the gold star.

The Baldrige Criteria contain the following basic categories for excellence (Baldrige, 2011-2012):

- Leadership
- Strategic planning
- Customer focus
- Measurement, analysis, and knowledge management
- Work force focus
- Operations focus
- Results

Like other performance frameworks, the Baldrige Criteria include leading indicators that help to drive the performance of each of the areas listed above. For example, promoting ethical behavior is an indicator of positive performance for a company. Employee training and succession planning of management are other leading indicators. These types of actions promote excellence and can indicate future productivity.

On the other hand, measuring results such as profits, levels of pollution, or resources used or lost are the outcomes of specific performance. These results are important and useful, but combining this information with leading indicators will provide a more complete picture of an organization's performance and potential.

Managing the Results

Some well-accepted indicators for measuring performance of sustainability are available, including the Global Reporting Initiative (GRI) as well as a variety of environmental, social, and governance (ESG) metrics used by the investment community. These metrics will be covered in more detail in future chapters. For now, it is helpful to know that any sustainability program should incorporate the measurement of results as well as future indicators (as provided by performance frameworks).

Using a sustainability management system and its sustainability footprint feature, an organization can determine the risks that the operation faces in the short term and in the long term. A program is put into place to address these risks as well as opportunities for improvement. As results are measured and analyzed, modifications can be made to drive continual improvement. By including management as well as employees at all levels, the sustainability program becomes systemic within the organization—*mainstreamed.*

The steps required to make this happen will be outlined in the chapters that follow. This book will show how mainstreaming corporate sustainability can become a part of what every employee looks forward to on a daily basis.

Supplementary Reading Suggestions

The end of each chapter will include additional reading recommendations for those of you wishing to delve more deeply into a particular topic. As mentioned in the preface, the goal of this book is to provide an overview of corporate sustainability as well as a firm foundation from which to build your own understanding. This is a rich field with many resources available, but it can become overwhelming without a few guideposts along the way. Hopefully, this book will provide a few signs and signals to help guide you on your journey.

To begin, you might want to take a look at the ISO website (http://www.iso.org/iso/home.html). This is a global organization that has published standards of practice in many different areas. The most commonly recognized is the ISO 14000 series of standards, *Environmental Management*. But ISO provides many other standards on many subjects, customized to various industries. The numbering system can be frustrating for the first-time user. Keep in mind that this is an international system. The numbers are intended to overcome potential language barriers. In addition, ISO provides various standards subsets, which focus on particular industries. The numbers used therefore allow for a more precise delineation of the various standards.

ISO standards documentation must be purchased. As such, they will not be reproduced here. However, there are many free summaries of the various standards available on the Internet, so it's easy to get an idea of what a standard is all about without making a purchase. If your company does decide to pursue a particular standard, they are available for roughly $150 to $300.

A wonderful article was published in the *Harvard Business Review* on the importance of transparency for modern companies, which describes how what seems like an externality can become an important internal concern for companies. The article provides a good introduction to the challenges of balancing the three areas of responsibility (i.e., environmental stewardship, social welfare, and economic prosperity).

> Meyer, C. & Kirby, J. (2010). Leadership in the age of transparency. *Harvard Business Review, 88*(4), 39-46.

There are also two excellent books on the subject of sustainability that go into greater detail than I have here. Both are included as recommended reading for the Corporate Sustainability Strategy class mentioned in the preface.

> Blackburn, W. (2007). *The sustainability handbook*. Washington, DC: Environmental Law Institute.

The Blackburn book is a comprehensive treatise on the subject, outlining in more detail many of the concepts covered here. In addition, the second half of the book is comprised of appendices including sample forms and tables to be used in practice, lists and explanations of various standards and their application, as well as other resources and organizations available to support and advise the sustainability professional. I highly recommend this resource.

> Googins, B., Mirvis, P, & Rochlin, S. (2007). *Beyond good company; next generation corporate citizenship*. New York: Palgrave MacMillan.

This book focuses on the social responsibility aspect of sustainability, which makes it a nice complement to the Blackburn book, which emphasizes environmental responsibility. The authors of the above text provide numerous examples of companies that have enhanced their performance and brand equity by improving their performance from a social equity perspective. It is an interesting read and also provides good support for the professional seeking to build a business case for social welfare in a company and throughout the supply chain.

References

Baldrige Performance Excellence Program (Baldrige). (2011-2012). *Criteria for performance excellence*. Gaithersberg, Md: National Institute of Standards and Technology.

Bärlund, K. (2004-2005). Sustainable development – concept and action. United Nations Economic Commission for Europe. Retrieved from: http://www.unece.org/oes/nutshell/2004-2005/focus_sustainable_development.html

Blackburn, W. (2007). *The sustainability handbook*. Washington, DC: Environmental Law Institute.

Cooperrider, D. & Whitney, D. (2005). *Appreciative inquiry*. San Francisco: Berrett-Koehler Publishers.

Environmental Leader, LLC. (2011). 2011 Insider knowledge: lessons learned from corporate environmental, sustainability, and energy decision-makers. Retrieved from http://www.environmentalleader.com/

Environmental Leader, LLC. (2012). 2012 Insider knowledge: lessons learned from corporate environmental, sustainability, and energy decision-makers. Retrieved from http://www.environmentalleader.com/

International Organization of Standards (ISO). 2009. ISO 26000: Guidance on social responsibility. Available from: http://www.iso.org/iso/home/standards.htm

United Nations. (1948). The universal declaration of human rights. Retrieved from http://www.un.org/en/documents/udhr/index.shtml

Chapter 2

The Corporation Perspective

It takes twenty years to build a reputation and five minutes to ruin it.
—Warren Buffet

The Rise of Corporations

Corporations have an enormous impact on our lives. There are 5.6 million corporations in the United States today, and although corporations make up only about 20 percent of the total number of businesses in the country, they comprise over 80 percent of total sales revenues (Pride, 2010, p. 116). To give you an idea of their overall power, of the largest one hundred economies in the world, it is estimated that thirty-seven are corporations. The United States, Japan, and China still dwarf even the largest corporation from a value-added standpoint, but ExxonMobil and Walmart are within the top fifty (DeGrauwe, 2002).[1]

Globalization as a result of multinational corporations is becoming increasingly apparent. Corporations wield an exceptional amount of control over global economies. The effect of corporations on people of all races and incomes will be part of what we examine in this book.

---

[1] This computation is based upon an estimation of "value added" provided by corporations as compared to national gross domestic product (GDP). Other estimates of corporate size have been conducted comparing sales revenues to GDP, but De Grauwe and Cameraman argue that since GDP is based upon value added, using sales revenues results in double counting of production for corporations by a factor of roughly 25 percent for manufacturing companies and 35 percent for service industries.

The earliest corporations were created by charter of the state, which allowed private financial resources to be utilized for governmental purposes. This enabled governments to expand their power around the world. Corporations were even utilized in war and in colonial expansion efforts.

The East India Company is one example of an early corporation. It was enlisted by the English to conquer and control much of India during colonial times. One advantage of using a corporate entity in such efforts was that liability for damages was limited to the amount invested in the company. The assets of individual investors, or the state itself, were therefore protected.

It is also interesting to note that Harvard College is the oldest corporate entity in the western hemisphere, founded in 1636 and incorporated in 1650 (http://www.admissionsconsultants.com/college/harvard.asp).

Corporate Monopolies

By the time Adam Smith wrote *The Wealth of Nations*, published in 1776, the effect of corporate monopolies on the market system had already become apparent. Smith was highly critical of concentrated ownership and its negative influences on competition. He warned that only after "suspicious attention" should policies recommended by corporations be considered. This is of even greater concern today, as we are confronted by concentrated ownership of mainstream media companies (Shah, 2002).

Concentrated corporate ownership and market monopolies enabled companies to set prices for their goods at unreasonably low levels to drive out competition. Some engaged in unfair trade practices. This caused great concern in American society, and in 1890, Congress passed the Sherman Antitrust Act to attempt to control some of these practices. The act specifically prohibited attempts to create a monopoly as well as contracts or conspiracies to restrain commerce or trade (Hovenkamp, 2005, p. 147).

But has antitrust legislation been enough? Because of the growth of multinational corporations and globalization, corporations have been able to sidestep antitrust legislation. Continued deregulation, trade liberalization, and privitization of industries such as utilities have given rise to powerful conglomerates that have outstripped the regulatory ability of individual governments. International organizations such as the World Trade Organization have been unable to provide adeqate relief (Robins, 2006, p. 185).

Benefits of Large Corporations

In spite of the criticism, large corporations do offer some advantages. The ability to manufacture products around the world has reduced the price of many consumer items such as televisions and appliances. In addition, customers can expect a certain quality of product in various regions. One example is McDonalds, which has over thirty thousand locations in 120 countries offering similar food and standards in each location (though one may argue that theirs is not necessarily a high enough standard).

Wages at larger corporations also tend to be higher, especially in firms with more than five hundred employees. Workers there are also more likely to be offered health insurance and fringe benefits than in smaller companies. Large companies that have been in existence for decades are less likely to file for bankruptcy (although there are some notable exceptions, such as United Airlines and Kmart). Investors are therefore more attracted to these companies given the expectation for more stable returns.

Finally, many large corporations support charitable causes in a big way (Roach, 2008). Is this just window dressing used to distract consumers from the lack of real effort made toward social or environmental sustainability?

The Flip Side...

Multinational corporations tend to establish subsidiaries in foreign countries where labor laws are less restrictive and wages are lower. Developing countries may even offer incentives to these companies to encourage foreign investment. Along the US–Mexico border, for example, multinational corporations have built factories in tax-free industrial zones, allowing for cheap production of goods that can then be exported back into the United States without tariffs. Though this may seem like an opportunity for employment using local labor, it denies needed tariff revenues to Mexico.

Although some argue that developing countries benefit from increased economic activity and employment, standards for environmental protection and working conditions in these countries are often inferior to those in developed countries. Multinational corporations are able to produce goods at a lower cost with the dual effect of keeping labor costs lower in their home country while circumventing minimum wage laws in developing countries. This has driven a debate concerning the conflicting issues of efficiency and fairness and the imbalance of economic growth and social injustice (Monshipouri, 2003).

Corporations and the Environment

Although many corporations strive to operate responsibly with respect to the environment, many concerns and criticisms of multinational corporations remain regarding their use of energy, treatment of toxic waste, and resource management. These concerns are particularly evident in the developing world, where laws and regulations can be lax or unevenly enforced.

The United Nations (UN) has made efforts over the past decades to resolve some of these issues, but not always with a positive effect. A UN project during the late 1990s aimed at improving corporate responsibility for human rights and environmental protection received considerable criticism because it involved many of the very corporations that had caused some of the most severe problems. Although it helped these corporations improve their image, it apparently accomplished little with respect to the underlying problems (Shah, Corporations and the Environment, 2002).

In 2002, the United Nations Environment Programme (UNEP) reported, "The state of the planet's environment is worsening, yet in most industry sectors only a few companies are striving for sustainability. For the rest, it is business as usual" (UNEP, 2002, p. 22).

The responsibility of corporations operating in nation states where environmental protections are minimal is part of an international debate. For example, in 1993, Shell was confronted with a large but nonviolent protest by a tribe in Nigeria. Oil production had devastated their tribal lands, and any money for renewal or compensation had disappeared into the hands of the corrupt military junta. When the tribal leader was arrested, Shell stood aside and did nothing to prevent the leader's execution (Scherer & Palazzo, 2007, p. 10).

Other examples include the hiring of scientists and advertising by Exxon to influence public opinion and policy decisions regarding climate change (Rowlands, 2000). Biotech industries have also been criticized for promoting genetically engineered food for profit motives rather than as a means to resolve the root causes of world hunger (Sherlock, 2002).

The rise of consumer interest in environmental issues has driven corporations to pay greater attention to environmental responsibility, but in some cases, their response has been primarily lip service versus real progress. Earthday Resources published an annual Don't Be Fooled Award until 2002 and since then other organizations have taken up the charge. Leading companies on the list include BP (this was before the 2010 Gulf oil spill), Shell, Ford Motor Company, Monsanto, Dow, and DuPont (http://www.corpwatch.org/article.php?id=943).

Corporate Social Responsibility

The debate over corporate social responsibility includes arguments from free-market capitalists contending that profits are king and that any limitations on profits would be detrimental to the free market's ability to naturally reward those companies who are most responsible.

On the other side, environmental and social activists contend that large corporations can assuage critics with token contributions to NGOs and other nonprofit groups along with publicity through media events, belying their resource use, toxic waste practices, and social abuses (Shah A. , 2007).

Ranking Countries on Social Responsibility

Table 2.1 below shows a ranking of countries that comprise the top 95 percent of global GDP spanning all five continents. It was compiled by the nonprofit group AccountAbility. Not surprisingly, the more advanced countries of the world are ranked at the top.

Table 2.1: Responsible Competitiveness Index (Zadek, 2007)

Country	Rank
Sweden	1
Denmark	2
Finland	3
Iceland	4
United Kingdom	5
Norway	6
New Zealand	7
Ireland	8
Australia	9
Canada	10
Germany	11
Netherlands	12
Switzerland	13
Belgium	14
Singapore	15
Austria	16
France	17
United States	18
Japan	19
Hong Kong, China	20

Developed countries are commonly criticized for moving many of their "dirty" industries to developing countries where regulations are less stringent. The AccountAbility report points out this issue, noting as an example, "up to 40 percent of air pollutants in the Pearl River Delta in low-scoring China are directly linked to exports to high-scoring importers across Europe and North America" (Zadek, 2007).

Indeed, a rather disturbing quote from former Harvard President Larry Summers, when he was Chief Economist for the World Bank, illustrates this problem. The following statement is quoted from an internal memo (Shiva, 2000, p. 65):

> Just between you and me, shouldn't the World Bank be encouraging more migration of dirty industries to the LDCs [less developed countries]?...The economic logic behind dumping a load of toxic waste in the lowest wage country is impeccable and we should face up to that...Under-populated countries in Africa are vastly under-polluted; their air quality is probably vastly inefficiently low compared to Los Angeles or Mexico City...The concern over an agent that causes a one in a million change in the odds of prostate cancer is obviously going to be much higher in a country where people survive to get prostate cancer than in a country where under-five mortality is two hundred per thousand.

Corporate Economic Responsibility

The most obvious responsibility of a corporation is economic responsibility. For public corporations, this includes paying its suppliers and employees, operating at a profit, and providing dividends to its shareholders as well as generating capital appreciation in the value of its stock.

Problems arise when corporations push the boundaries of existing laws to drive stock prices up. A number of scandals in this area have taken place in recent years, conflicts primarily driven by corporate executives who were issued stock or stock options as part of their compensation packages. This provided a temptation to inflate profits thereby driving stock prices up so that these executives could sell their stock at inflated prices. Ordinary investors, in contrast, suffered large losses when the company's true financial situation eventually became public.

Many economists at the end of the twentieth century supported the practice of dispensing stock options in addition to salary as a means of executive compensation, arguing that linking stock prices to compensation would encourage executives to manage the corporation wisely, therefore producing a benefit for all shareholders. Unfortunately, executives with large stock holdings had an incentive to temporarily inflate the company's stock price allowing them to take advantage of their options and sell their stock at a higher price. Some companies used complex accounting schemes to keep losses and liabilities off the company's books such that profits appeared higher than they actually were.

In the case of WorldCom, the company's profits were found to be overstated by $4 billion. The stock price fell from a high of over sixty dollars per share to just pennies after the deception was revealed. Enron is another example, probably the most famous, thanks in part to the fast-paced culture of greed and influence unveiled at the highest levels of government (Roach, 2008).

Corporate Perspective—Three Responsibilities

As we think about the three areas of corporate responsibility—environmental, social, and economic—it is also important to think about how a corporation looks at the world versus how the world looks at corporations. Some people look at the three areas of responsibility and see all of the bad things that corporations do, such as degradation of the environment including emissions and toxins, mistreatment of employees, and avoidance of taxes or other regulations. If you take this perspective, corporate responsibility can feel like a very discouraging situation.

However, it is important for a corporation to understand the impacts that it has on the world—*looking out*—and to see the impacts that it has on the environment, the economy, and society. A more proactive approach is to *look internally*, or within a corporation, and to try to improve what is under the corporation's control. For example, a corporation can choose to use resources wisely, to reduce waste, and to manage their profits responsibly.

One way to look at this is to shift from an attitude of "take, make, waste" to "borrow, use, return." A corporation should have a goal to control everything in the plant from this perspective. If all of the resources stay in the plant and no waste or toxins are released, sustainability is achieved. Of course, this is never completely possible, but it is a good vision or goal for any operation.

Figure 2.1, below, shows an image of how this perspective might be visualized.

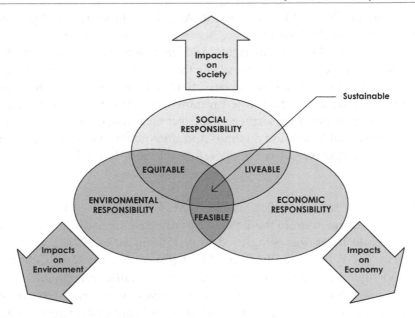

**Figure 2.1: Corporate Perspective on the Three Responsibilities,
Looking In and Looking Out**

Top-Down versus Bottom-Up

In this book, we will look at corporations that are organized and operated from a top-down management perspective. Multinational corporations control business units that are spread around the world, both in different countries and on different continents. Their supply chains stretch to facilities of all sizes and levels, including individual farmers and producers. Top-down management is therefore very important for larger corporations.

Engaging a corporation's employees at all levels is also necessary for full implementation of sustainability. For smaller companies, a more fluid bottom-up and top-down combination is more effective, as the facilities are smaller and personal communication between management and the work force can more easily be facilitated.

Trade Justice

Problems with trade justice (or injustice) abound with multinational corporations. Trade agreements such as the North American Free Trade

Agreement (NAFTA), the Central American Free Trade Agreement (CAFTA), and the Free Trade Agreement of the Americas have loosened trade barriers, but human rights and environmental protections have remained lax. Concepts such as "fair trade" versus "free trade" are gaining ground, but it is a slow process. Starbucks was stung by its venture into fair trade coffee and now promotes its Coffee and Farmer Equity program that provides farmers with technical assistance to implement more sustainable farming methods and microloans, and pays a premium price to its growers. It is not a perfect solution, but it is a start (Gans, 2006).

Examples of trade injustice are not hard to find, some of which include beverage companies. In the 1990s, cases of abuse were discovered in Brazil as child labor was being used to pick oranges. In 1996, Tropicana (a division of PepsiCo) and Minute Maid (owned by the Coca-Cola Company) signed pledges to discontinue using Brazilian orange juice. Some companies have continued to use Brazilian juices and have gotten around the United States Food and Drug Administration restriction by importing juice concentrate (Talley, 1999).

Another beverage example is the growth in popularity of the berry guarana, noted for its energy and stimulation qualities and used in drinks such as SoBe (owned by PepsiCo) and Rockstar Energy Drink. The entry of multinational corporations into this market has depressed the price of the guarana berry to local producers by as much as 80 percent. This has resulted in a series of legal claims over trademark to the Guarana name. Coca-Cola has now stepped into the fray and invested in genetic engineering to improve the plant's productivity (DeMello, 2005).

Criticism for Fiji Water abounds. The following excerpt from *Mother Jones* is particularly strident (Lenzer, 2009):

> Nowhere in Fiji Water's glossy marketing materials will you find reference to the typhoid outbreaks that plague Fijians because of the island's faulty water supplies; the corporate entities that Fiji Water has—despite the owners' talk of financial transparency—set up in tax havens like the Cayman Islands and Luxembourg; or the fact that its signature bottle is made from Chinese plastic in a diesel-fueled plant and hauled thousands of miles to its eco-conscious consumers. And, of course, you won't find mention of

the military junta for which Fiji Water is a major source of global recognition and legitimacy.

The Big Picture—Corporate Assets: Buildings, Production, and the Supply Chain

Multinational corporations own various types of assets. These assets may include offices, manufacturing or production facilities, warehouses, distribution centers, retail stores, restaurants, mining or drilling operations, pipelines, and fleets of cars, trucks, or buses. At the same time, they may form subsidiaries or other corporate entities that are only partially owned by the parent company, but which perform duties for the parent company through contractual arrangements. In this section, we will compare just two companies—Coca-Cola and Pepsi—to give you some perspective as to the assets owned by a large corporation.

The Coca-Cola Company

The corporate headquarters of the Coca-Cola Company sits on a thirty-five-acre office complex in Atlanta, Georgia. It owns or leases properties all over the world for administration, production, storage, distribution, and sales of its beverage products. In North America, they own twenty-three facilities for still beverage, beverage concentrate, or bottled water production. Outside of North America they own and operate another twenty facilities. In addition, they own or have a majority interest in 112 beverage bottling or canning facilities around the world. Their net operating revenue for 2009 was $31 billion, with a net income of $6.8 billion, and total assets of $49 billion, with a little over $5 billion in long-term debt (Coca-Cola, 2010).

The Coca-Cola Company is separate, however, from many of the other bottling companies that bottle and can the beverages from concentrates made by Coca-Cola. Although Coca-Cola owns the brands and is responsible for marketing said brands, about 80 percent of the three hundred companies that bottle and can the products are independent or Coca-Cola holds a less than controlling equity interest in these companies. These companies are responsible for distribution and merchandising of the product to retailers around the world, including over two hundred countries. However, according to a website announcement, the Coca-Cola Company is in the process of negotiating with its largest US bottler, Coca-Cola Enterprises, to acquire the company in exchange for ownership in bottling companies in Norway, Sweden, and Germany. The move is seen as a way to streamline distribution, allowing for one delivery system to retailers of beverage concentrate for fountain drinks as well as bottled or canned beverages (Styne, 2010).

Coca-Cola also has a fairly substantial equity interest (ranging from 23 percent to 35 percent) in the next four largest bottling companies that handle distribution in the United States, Canada, and western Europe; Mexico; Eastern Europe; and the Pacific region (The Coca-Cola Company, 2007). With the current Coca-Cola Enterprises agreement under way, it will be interesting to see what direction Coca-Cola takes regarding the ownership of future interests in bottling operations.

PepsiCo, Inc.

PepsiCo, on the other hand, includes not only beverages but also food and snack companies, such as Quaker, Frito-Lay, Tropicana, Gatorade, and, of course, Pepsi. They make, market, and sell their products through wholly owned subsidiaries or through contractual arrangements, and operate in two hundred countries, the largest of which include the United States, Canada, Mexico, and the United Kingdom. Their main headquarters in North America is located in Purchase, New York. Their net operating revenue for 2009 was $43 billion, with a net income of almost $6 billion, total assets of roughly $40 billion, and long-term debt of $7.4 billion (PepsiCo, 2010). So, Coke and Pepsi are roughly the same size in terms of revenue, but Coke dominates the beverage industry while Pepsi is much more diversified in the food and beverage industry.

PepsiCo is organized into four major divisions that comprise its family of companies: PepsiCo Americas Beverages (the beverage business in North America); PepsiCo Americas Foods (foods and snacks in North and South America); PepsiCo Europe (both foods and beverages across Europe); as well as PepsiCo Middle East and Africa (both foods and beverages, using some of their own bottling plants).

In February 2010, PepsiCo merged with two of its major bottling companies in North America to form Pepsi Beverage Company, which controls about 75 percent of its bottling operations in the United States, Canada, and Mexico. In an interesting blog posting, industry analyst Bob Ferrari explains in more detail PepsiCo's move toward greater control of distribution and flexibility of its supply chain through this acquisition. He also discusses Coca-Cola's move to acquire its major bottling facilities in North America. A decision made in part due to pressure from retailers such as Walmart, this move allows both companies to be more responsive to market demands and also to realize value from the bottling operations (Ferrari, 2010).

Supply Chain

Supervision of supply chains has become an important issue for multinational corporations as globalization has led to the outsourcing of production to countries where labor is cheap. The result has been a race to the bottom of sorts, a pursuit for the least expensive production. This shift exploded in the early 1980s as reports surfaced of sweatshop conditions in factories making clothing for big brand companies. Reports of child labor in countries including Bangladesh, India, Pakistan, and Haiti led to consumer backlash and even class action lawsuits. Labor laws in many of these countries were either inadequate or unenforced as government inspectors did not enforce the rules protecting workers.

Initially, the industry responded by introducing various codes of conduct, which resulted in social and environmental standards audits that were typically based on International Labour Organization conventions and UN declarations. The most significant progress was made in health and safety as these issues were easier to address.

But issues concerning wages and working hours have proven more difficult to resolve. Paying the minimum wage in many countries did not equate to a living wage, and even though workers were paid overtime, many factories still employed seven-day workweeks in order to meet production quotas. Audits had their own issues as well, as workers were coached to provide the right answers, records were falsified, and auditors were bribed. Finally, as multiple audits from different brands descended upon the same supplier, "audit fatigue" became a problem in and of itself.

In the past decade, brands like Nike, Adidas, Levi's, and retailers including Walmart and Marks & Spencer have adopted a different tactic. They realized that it was more effective to *engage* their suppliers in productivity measures, including lean manufacturing and establishing sustainability management systems in the factories themselves. Certification models such as ISO's social accountability standard (SA8000) and the Worldwide Responsible Accredited Production have been used to provide a framework for these improvements.

The change has not been easy, however. For a company like Adidas, with over 1,100 factories in sixty-eight countries, getting these practices into every factory can be a daunting task. Nike has six hundred supplier factories in more than fifty countries and indirectly employs about one million workers. Some brands have started to work together to create an industry-wide monitoring framework and education program. Walmart, Gap, and Timberland, along with a number of their suppliers, as one example, initiated a multi-stakeholder collaboration. These companies have formed a monitoring program in Cambodia, which they hope to expand into other developing countries.

By collaborating with suppliers rather than coercing them, these companies have begun to make headway. Using peer-to-peer engagement among suppliers has been the focus of UK retailer Marks & Spencer, which has set a goal to become the world's most sustainable major retailer by 2015. They are working to establish model factories in Sri Lanka, Bangladesh, and China, providing training to workers and supervisors to improve labor relations. Their goal is to improve productivity in the factories so that the savings can be passed along to the workers. Using a "balanced scorecard" of various social, environmental, and economic metrics, they are working toward implementing better practices within their factories.

Stakeholders continue to raise the bar higher, however. Clothing industries are under pressure by consumers and NGOs to move further down the supply chain to improve how their raw materials are cultivated and harvested. Besides a reduction in energy and water use, more sustainable agricultural practices have also become a concern (Chhabara, 2010).

More Supply Chain Examples

For Coca-Cola, the supply chain for the main company consists primarily of the products used to create the concentrates for its brands' beverages. Upstream suppliers include producers of high fructose corn syrup, sucrose, various fruit juices, artificial sweeteners, and colorants. Downstream in the supply chain are the bottling and canning operations, including plastic bottles and aluminum cans, as well as warehousing and distribution to grocery stores, movie theatres, restaurants, and the multitude of outlets that sell Coca-Cola products. Figure 2.2 below shows a basic supply chain outline.

Figure 2.2: Supply Chain Outline

For PepsiCo, the supply chain is even more complex as their products include food and snack items as well as beverages. Think of the complexity of their contracts with various agricultural producers from around the world. Imagine how far in advance they must work to maintain an adequate supply and how they must balance that supply with anticipated consumer demand. Packaging and distribution is more complicated as well given the various boxes and bags plus distribution to a variety of retail outlets.

Both PepsiCo and Coca-Cola have supply chain strategies and policies for environmental protection as well as social responsibility. We will examine these types of policies further as we delve into the supply chain later in the book.

Conclusion

After considering each of these factors for a multinational corporation, how can one even contemplate moving such a behemoth toward a more sustainable existence? In this book, we will investigate the various tools available to assist large corporations toward more responsible management of their businesses. The pressure from stakeholders for increased transparency, fair labor practices around the world, better resource management, and equitable representation of women in the work force have all come to the forefront in recent years. Further, the Internet has made much of this information readily available to stakeholders around the world. It is a very exciting time.

Supplementary Reading Suggestions

There are a number of lists you can consult regarding the size of various corporations. *Fortune* publishes an annual report of the largest five hundred global companies based on annual revenue on their website:

http://money.cnn.com/magazines/fortune/fortune500/

The UN Conference on Trade and Development also publishes lists on their website using various criteria including a geographical spread index:

http://unctad.org/

References

Butler, R. (2005, July 18). *Corporations among largest global economic entities, rank above many countries.* Retrieved July 12, 2010 from Mongabay.com:
http://news.mongabay.com/2005/0718-worlds_largest.html

Chhabara, R. (2010, July/August). Briefing: Supply Chains. *Ethical Corporation,* pp. 11-19.

Corporation. (2010). Retrieved July 12, 2010 from Wikipedia:
http://en.wikipedia.org/wiki/Corporations

De Bettignies, H. & Lepineux, F. (2009). Can multinational corporations afford to ignore the common good? *Business and Society Review ,* 142 (2), 153-182.

De Grauwe, P. & Camerman, P. (2002). How big are the big multinational companies? *Tijdshrift Voor Economie en Management, 47* (3), 311-326.

DeMello, I. E. (2005). Guarana - Prospects and geographic indicator status. *TED Case Studies ,* 780 .

Ferrari, B. (2010, Mar 3). *Supply change structural change begins to emerge within the beverages industry.* Retrieved July 28, 2010 from Supply Chain Matters:
http://www.theferrarigroup.com/blog1/tag/coca-cola-supply-chain/

Gans, J. (2006, Nov 11). *How fair is starbucks?* Retrieved July 26, 2010 from Core Economics: http://economics.com.au/?p=488

Hovenkamp, H. (2005). Exclusion and the Sherman Act. *The University of Chicago Law Review ,* 72 (1), 147.

Lenzer, A. (2009, Aug 17). *Fiji water: spin the bottle.* Retrieved July24, 2010 from http://www.corpwatch.org/article.php?id=15427

Monshipouri, M. W. (2003, Nov). Multinational corporations and the ethics of global responsibility: problems and possibilities. *Human Rights Quarterly ,* 25(4).

PepsiCo, I. (2010, Feb 22). *10-K annual report.* Retrieved July 27, 2010 from Edgar Online: http://yahoo.brand.edgar-online.com/displayfilinginfo.aspx?FilingID=7070460-226947-231828&type=sect&dcn=0001193125-10-036385

Roach, B. (2008, November). *Social and environmental responsibility of corporations.* (M. Toffel, Ed.) Retrieved July 24, 2010 from The Encylopedia of Earth:

http://www.eoearth.org/article/Social_and_environmental_responsibi
liy_of_corporations

Robins, N. (2006). *The corporation that changed the world: how the East India
Company shaped the modern multinational.* Pluto Press.

Rowlands, I. H. (2000). Beauty and the beast? BP's and Exxon's positions on
global climate change. Environment and Planning.

Scherer, A. G. & Palazzo, G. (2008, Mar). Globalization and corporate social
responsibility. *The Oxford Handbook of Corporate Social Responsibility .*
Oxford University Press.

Shah, A. (2007). *Corporate social responsibility.* Retrieved July 25, 2010 from Global
Issues: http://www.globalissues.org/article/723/corporate-social-
responsibility

Shah, A. (2002, May 25). *Corporations and the environment.* Retrieved July 12, 2010
from Global Issues:
http://www.globalissues.org/article/55/corporations-and-the-
environment

Shah, A. (2002, December 05). *The rise of corporations.* Retrieved July 5, 2010 from
Global Issues: http://www.globalissues.org/article/234/the-rise-of-
corporations

Sherlock, R. & Morrey, J. (2002). *Ethical issue in biotechnology.* Lanham, MD:
Rohman & Littlefield Publishers, Inc.

Sherman Antitrust Act. (2010). Retrieved July 12, 2010 from Wikipedia:
http://en.wikipedia.org/wiki/Sherman_Antitrust_Act

Shiva, V. (2000). *Stolen harvest.* South End Press.

Styne, T. & Cordeiro, A. (2010, Mar 29). *Coca-Cola names supply-chain executive to
lead integration.* Retrieved July 28, 2010 from Fox Business:
http://www.foxbusiness.com/story/markets/industries/retail/updat
e-coca-cola-names-supply-chain-executive-lead-integration/

Talley, N. (1999). Sweet oranges? *TED Case Studies .*

The Coca-Cola Company. (2007). *2007 Annual review.* Retrieved July 28, 2010
from The Coca-Cola Company: http://www.thecoca-
colacompany.com/citizenship/the_coca-cola_system.html

The Coca-Cola Company. (2010, Feb 26). *Form 10-K.* (The Coca-Cola Company,
Producer, & Securities and Exchange Commission) Retrieved July 27,
2910 from Securities and Exchange Commission:
http://www.sec.gov/Archives/edgar/data/317540/0001193125060561
63/d10k.htm#toc50951_4

The rise of the corporation, Chapter 7. (N.D.). Retrieved July 12, 2010 from
http://www.delmarlearning.com/companions/content/140187083x/p
pt/Ch7.ppt

The state of the planet is getting worse but for many it's still "business as usual".
(2002). Retrieved July 14, 2010 from UNEP:
http://www.unep.org/Documents.Multilingual/Default.asp?Documen
tID=248&ArticleID=3049

UNCTAD. (n.d.). From UN Committee on Trade & Development; Multinational
Corporations (MNCs) in Least Developed Countries (LDCs):
www.unc.edu/~wwolford/Geog21Spring2004/UNCTAD.pdf

UNEP. (2002). *UNEP in 2002.* Retrieved July 24, 2010 from
http://www.unep.org/publications/contents/pub_details_search.asp?
ID=274

Zadek, S. & MacGillivray, A. (2007, July). The state of responsible
competitiveness 2007. London: AccountAbility

Chapter 3

Business Case for Sustainability

I think that the world has reached a tipping point now. We're beyond the debates over whether [addressing sustainability] is something that needs to be done or not—it's now mostly about how we do it. And from the perspective of ecomagination, it's not about altruism; it's about creating value.

—Steve Fludder, Vice President, ecomagination, General Electric

Business Case Questions

Any discussion of corporate environmental and social responsibility inevitably lands on the business case for sustainability. How do you justify any extra expenses required to change processes and policies in order to improve the impacts of your business on the environment and society? How do you calculate the overall benefits? What effect will these changes have on the overall profitability of the company? Will your shareholders object?

In spite of these questions, sustainability is clearly on the front burner for companies today. In fact, in a recent survey of the executives and managers of over 1,500 companies, 92 percent of the respondents stated that they were addressing sustainability at least in some way. At the same time, more than 70 percent said they had not yet developed a robust business case for sustainability (MIT & BCG, 2009).

These conflicting statistics illuminate the challenge for many businesses in fully accepting both how sustainability can drive performance and why a better understanding of the tools to achieve success is necessary. The less informed see sustainability as satisfying regulatory minimums.

Experts see sustainability as a value center for the business, an integral part of every decision (MIT & BCG, 2009). [2]

"Embracers" of sustainability can be seen as those who have solid commitment to sustainable practices in their operations and who are pushing those practices through their supply chains. They view sustainability as a pathway toward gaining a competitive edge and increasing market share (MIT & BCG, 2011). Figure 3.1 below shows the overlap among answers to three important sustainability questions. You can see that the majority of responders recognize the competitive advantage gained through sustainability and have permanently placed it on their agenda. But only the embracers exhibit a solid core of conviction, having developed a solid business case for sustainability.

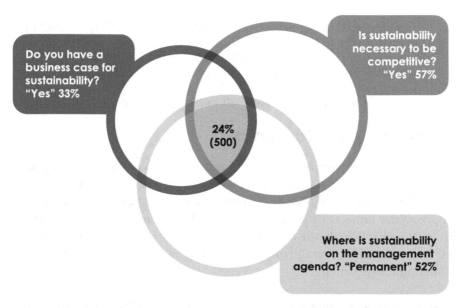

Do you have a business case for sustainability? "Yes" 33%

Is sustainability necessary to be competitive? "Yes" 57%

24% (500)

Where is sustainability on the management agenda? "Permanent" 52%

Figure 3.1: Embracers of Sustainability Answered Yes to All Three Questions
(MIT & BCG, 2011, p. 9)

Larger companies are adopting sustainability more quickly than smaller companies, although notable exceptions such as Patagonia and New Belgium brewery provide leading examples for smaller companies. Some larger companies like Clorox have purchased businesses such as Burt's

---

[2] The MIT & BCG survey was a diverse mix of for-profit companies, ranging in size from under ten thousand employees (69 percent) to over 100,000 employees (9 percent), including all regions of the world, with a wide variety of industries represented (MIT & BCG, 2009, p. 23).

Bees to learn more about how to adopt sustainability practices and make them a part of their own larger operations. Doing so also helps to expand their brand image in a positive way (MIT & BCG, 2011).

But building brand reputation around sustainability can create risk, as exemplified by the recent challenges faced by BP. Although their reputation rose after committing to investments in renewable energy, the disaster of Deepwater Horizon in the Gulf of Mexico in the summer of 2010 tarnished that image considerably. BP's response and future practices will certainly determine whether or not they can regain their former reputation.

Embracers Defining the Business Case

Embracers of sustainability are much more likely to have a solid business case definition for sustainability, often referring either to the Brundtland definition or the triple bottom line (or the balance of people, planet, and profit). Embracers are also much more likely to see the financial benefit of engaging in sustainability practices.

Overwhelmingly, embracers view improved corporate image as the primary benefit of sustainability. They also see it providing real results for their companies. Leaders in this field include well-known companies such as General Electric, IBM, Toyota, Walmart, and Royal Dutch Shell. But the list also includes other lesser-known companies such as Rio Tinto Group, International Watch Company, and Better Place (MIT & BCG, 2009).

The research results are in on performance, too. The financial performance of sustainably managed companies has been shown to positively correlate with their corporate responsibility (Waddock & Bodwell, 2007, p. 35.) The steps involved in managing a company responsibly necessitate thoughtful planning, careful record keeping, and results analysis. This is part of the plan-do-check-act cycle that many environmental management systems dictate. We will cover these ideas in more detail in Chapter 11. Having a strong management system that includes environmental and social responsibility controls drives a company toward better financial success. More and more companies are realizing this, as the MIT & BCG surveys have shown.

Those companies that have not embraced the business case for sustainability represent where the greatest benefits can be applied. Starting a "green team" or developing a series of initiatives can provide some benefits, but doing so can also result in failure without the assurance of overall commitment. Success is driven by a whole system approach to embedding sustainability throughout a company. This is a continuing theme in sustainability.

Connecting Vision with Value

The leading companies that are succeeding in sustainability have successfully made the connection between financial benefit and sustainable practices. They are driving these values into their supply chains and even selecting suppliers based on these values. With long-term planning and focus on the ultimate sustainability goals, these companies are able to formulate holistic plans, balancing costs across various organization areas and funding projects that may not otherwise receive approval. Recognizing the overall value of investment in reducing waste in one area can be the deciding factor regarding whether or not to move forward on a project.

In Chapter 2, Nike and Adidas were provided as examples regarding labor practices in developing countries. Nike also revised its business plan regarding material waste in the 1990s and developed a customized business case to fit with its own values in order to drive down the use of toxic materials and to produce cost savings. By evaluating their design procedures, they realized that for every two pairs of shoes manufactured, they were wasting enough materials to produce a third pair. Revising their processes not only reduced waste but also significantly improved their bottom line. This was made possible in part by their integration of Nike's overall values as well as their "just do it" mentality (MIT & BCG, 2009, p. 13).

Top Line, Bottom Line, or Both?

As the results of the MIT & BCG survey showed, many companies see the value of improving their brand image through sustainability as a means to improve their top line (revenue). They also see that reducing resource waste and improving worker productivity can improve the bottom line (profit).

A number of books have emerged in this field, including Esty and Winston's *Green to Gold* and Andrew Savitz's *The Triple Bottom Line*, both of which contain resources and case study examples relevant to any company choosing to build a business case for sustainability. Once again, the commonalities include cutting costs by increasing resource efficiencies, increasing revenues by improving brand strength, reducing risk by improving reputation, as well as improving processes to control spills and leaks.

The key is to find the language that fits your company and then to involve leaders across the organization to ensure buy-in across the board. Driving both top-line and bottom-line returns will prove the naysayers wrong. There are fewer of them every day.

Show Me the Money Model

William Blackburn has written an extensive treatise on corporate sustainability called *The Sustainability Handbook* (2007). His model for the value of sustainability begins by asking if sustainability can be justified on purely financial terms. He argues that it can. By incorporating a Sustainability Management System (SMS) throughout an organization, he argues that a business can be made more productive and more profitable while still improving its impacts on the environment and on society (p. 36).

Blackburn presents seven key factors that drive profits and dividends. He then analyzes these factors in detail to show that each can have successful financial returns under the guidance of an SMS. The seven factors are listed below.

- Factor 1: *Reputation and brand strength*—One-fourth to one-third of a company's reputation is based upon its environmental and social performance (p. 39).

- Factor 2: *Competitive, effective, and desirable products, services, and new markets*—Companies can improve their market share by spurring creative innovations that include sustainable objectives thereby increasing sales and profits (p. 49).

- Factor 3: *Productivity*—Many sustainability aspects include increased efficiencies, which naturally reduce costs and increase profitability (p. 70).

- Factor 4: *Operational burden and interference*—A company that embraces sustainability reduces its risk of public distrust and higher public scrutiny (p. 83).

- Factor 5: *Supply chain costs*—Working with suppliers in a proactive manner reduces the risk of supply chain interruption and ensures that costs are controlled (p. 86).

- Factor 6: *Cost of capital (lender and investor appeal)*—A growing number of investors are making their decisions based not only on financial terms but also on social and environmental performance (p. 89).

- Factor 7: *Legal liability*—Companies that address sustainability are much less likely to be tripped up by legal liabilities that can wipe out precious profits (p. 98).

Overall, Blackburn argues that although each of these factors can provide financial benefit, they also provide intangible environmental and social benefits. Making the right decisions in each area demands a broad perspective and requires balancing the various concerns of stakeholders involved. Ultimately, the decision needs to be driven by the company's overall vision (2007, p. 103).

Sometimes, those decisions can be counterintuitive. When Henry Ford doubled his workers' wages to five dollars in 1913 and shortened the workday from nine hours to eight hours, his critics howled. But in effect, his modifications greatly improved productivity by cutting worker turnover. As Ford said at the time, "If you cut wages, you just cut the number of your customers." The net result: Ford's business boomed (Ford Motor Co.).

Potential Bottom-Line Benefits

Sustainability can also significantly increase productivity in the work force. Bob Willard, former IBM executive turned sustainability guru, argues that an inspired work force can drive sustainability throughout a company as they contribute to finding more ways to improve revenue, create eco-efficiencies, and drive innovations that improve the bottom line, while also improving the working environment. Table 3.1 below shows Willard's analysis of the various potential savings and benefits.

Table 3.1: Comparison of Business Case Elements
(Willard, 2009, p. 29)

Seven Business Case Benefits	Improvement Possible	Sustainability Business Case Components
Reduced recruiting costs	-1.0%	Corporate reputation and enhanced brand image
Reduced attrition costs	-2.0%	Employee morale and productivity/elevate employee awareness of sustainability
Increased productivity	+10.5%	Employee morale and productivity/elevate employee awareness of sustainability Stimulate innovation and generate new ideas
Reduced expenses in manufacturing	-5.0%	Ensure continual improvement Cost savings
Reduced water, energy, and consumables expenses	-20.0%	Cost savings
Increased revenue and market share	+5.0%	Access to markets and customers/customer loyalty Expedited permitting/improved relations with regulators
Reduced risk/easier financing	-5.0%	Reduce and manage business risks Earn and maintain a social license to operate Improved relations with stakeholders/dispute resolution/issues management Establish or improve reputation with investors, bond agencies, and banks
Total Potential Profit Increase of 38%		

Shared Value

Michael Porter introduced the concept of "shared value" wherein a corporation's economic and social responsibilities overlap and are complementary. He published an article in the *Harvard Business Review* with Mark Kramer (Porter & Kramer, 2011) that describes how many leading companies have recognized the importance of shared value and

how real benefits to the bottom line can be unleashed from sharing corporate largesse with local communities that supply the company's mate-
materials.

Porter and Kramer use Nestlé as an example, a company that has
worked with impoverished coffee growers to increase their productivity.
Nestlé provides education, planting stock, fertilizers, and also guaran-
tees prices thereby improving the quality and quantity of coffee and also
reducing the environmental impact of the farms. It was a win–win for
both the company and the local communities. Other companies like General Motors, Walmart, Unilever, and Johnson & Johnson have conducted
similar programs. Porter and Kramer see this as a model for spurring
innovation and creativity as well as a new way to solve difficult global
social problems.

Risk Management

Corporations are increasingly characterizing their actions in terms of risk
and risk management, and this risk assessment applies to environmental,
social, and economic responsibilities as well. Increasing brand value
through sustainability practices can have significant, positive effects for a
company, but it can also backfire. For Toyota, their positive "green"
brand reputation was damaged by the recall of the Prius model. For
Royal Dutch Shell, their reputation was damaged by the overall challenges faced by the oil industry after the BP Deepwater Horizon disaster.

How a company addresses these challenges—proactively facing up to
them, denying the charges, or taking a defensive posture—can impact
the resiliency of their brand. Many sustainability professionals argue that
openness and transparency are a much better approach in the long run,
and that stakeholders are quick to react when they see even a hint of
"greenwashing." Woe to the company who pretends to be perfect!

Many guidelines and standards are available to help companies address
risk, one of which is the ISO 31000 risk management standard. This
standard outlines the areas that a company should address to make certain it is protecting itself from bad risks as well as taking advantage of
opportunities or *good* risks. The investment community in particular will
benefit from this ISO standard as it addresses the environmental, social,
and governance (commonly referred to as ESG) concerns that are of great
importance to them.

The ISO 31000 risk management system can be incorporated into an organization's overall SMS. It can also be customized to fit the organization's vision and goals. The ISO 31000 outline includes understanding the organization and its context; establishing a risk management policy; integration of the risk management policy into the company's processes; committing adequate resources to policy implementation; and monitoring and reviewing progress for continual improvement (ISO, 2009, p. iii).

Once again, driving this system into and throughout the company, or *mainstreaming* its guidelines, will enable the company to make sustainability part of what every employee does every day. Roles and responsibilities for each employee and each department will be guided by the management system, a system that incorporates flexibility to make sure that innovation and creativity are encouraged. Management systems demand continuous improvement. The plan-do-check-act cycle is a continuous loop, one that demands self-assessment along the way, driving quality and preventing harm (thereby satisfying risk reduction).

Economic Downturn + Government Inaction = Sustainability Investment

A surprising conclusion of the 2011 MIT & BCG survey showed that in spite of the economic downturn beginning in late 2008, most companies (59 percent) are currently increasing their investments in sustainability. Almost 70 percent said they expect to make even further increases in the future. In contrast, only 25 percent said they were spending less on sustainability measures (p. 7). The writers note that this investment seems to come in the face, or perhaps in response to, the lack of governmental policy progress at the climate change talks in Copenhagen and more recently at the Rio+20 talks.

Rio+20 was a huge disappointment for the environmental community from a government standpoint, but there are many who say that significant progress was made among the corporations and NGOs in attendance. Paul Polman, CEO of Unilever, admitted that the final text of the negotiations was a "race to the bottom," but that there were clusters of companies and countries who showed commitment to changing the way business is run around the globe. Polman stated as follows (Confino, 2012):

> Amongst business there is now a critical mass forming around deforestation and energy for all, as companies say we cannot continue like this. We are entering a very interesting period of history where the responsible business world is running ahead of the politicians. The political climate is very difficult and to some extent paralyzed. Over the next two to three years, I believe there will be enough critical mass with groups of countries and companies starting tangible projects. As with many change programs, when you create some success around some specific tangible projects, it will attract others. There are leaders and followers and laggards in everything.

As with the MIT & BCG embracers versus cautious adopters, the embracers are leading the charge and driving innovation, pulling the rest of the field along. The cautious adopters will need to catch up or they may be left hopelessly behind.

Customizing the Business Case

Every company needs to adapt its reasoning for sustainability to fit with its own operations, culture, and vision. But this doesn't have to be done in a vacuum.

There are many guides and tools available, but one resource that is very clearly written and that has been well vetted was developed by the SIGMA Project in 2003. The Sustainability Integrated Guidelines for Management (SIGMA) Project was organized in 1999 with the support of the UK Department of Trade and Industry. It was led by three organizations: the British Standards Institution, a leading standards organization; Forum for the Future, a leading sustainability charity and think tank; and AccountAbility, an international professional body for accountability.

The SIGMA Business Case Tool (2003) offers a clear step-by-step process for customizing a business case for an organization. It includes links to other SIGMA publications and planning documents to provide a more robust planning process.

The SIGMA Business Case Tool outlines a five-step process (p. 3-4):

1. Understand the significant impacts
2. Identify key stakeholder issues
3. Make it relevant (link opportunities and risks from 1 and 2)
4. Back it up (provide examples and data)
5. Keep it dynamic and updated (make sure organizational priorities are updated and are connected to processes)

In addition to these basic steps, the Business Case Tool contains a chart plus examples of impact areas, risks, and opportunities. It is this type of tool that can help an organization get started, helping to analyze its business case and develop a comprehensive SMS.

Challenges

The 2009 MIT & BCG survey uncovered three main challenges faced by companies adopting a business case. They include (p. 17):

1. *Developing forecasting that goes beyond a typical one- to five-year time frame:* Many companies are focused on the short term, even quarterly returns, and for many sustainability efforts, a longer-term perspective is needed.
2. *Understanding and measuring the overall effects of their efforts:* Some companies struggle to identify and measure (and then control) even the tangible effects of their sustainability efforts, let alone the intangible ones. Those serious about sustainability are willing to find ways to quantify the less tangible effects and to gain a better understanding of the holistic effort.
3. *Being able to plan in an area of uncertainty:* Most traditional strategic planning results from analysis and prediction of effects after the implementation of certain strategies. For many sustainability efforts, the effects are less certain—future regulation, customer satisfaction, market demand, as examples—and so it takes a different kind of planning and strategy framework to implement these plans.

The MIT & BCG team recommend an updated framework to meet these challenges. Depicted in figure 3.2 below, it shows that various company objectives can be sorted among different timelines, thereby helping to prioritize and plan.

Time horizon of a sustainability effort

	Short Term	Long Term
Specific to a company (or industry)	**2. Good business practices** • Transparency • Supply chain productivity	**3. Competitive differentiation** • Product redesign • New market entry • New organizational models
Shared universally among all companies	**1. Table stakes** • Public relations • Compliance • Efficiencies	**4. Game-changing innovation for the future** • Reframed economic models • Partnerships with stakeholders

Drivers and impacts of a sustainability effort (vertical axis label)

Figure 3.2: Framework for Strategizing Business Case Objectives
(MIT & BCG, 2009, p. 16)

Finding Examples

Another excellent way to develop a business case is to read the sustainability reports of other companies—either competitors in the same industry or in other industries. After reading a number of these reports, you will be able to discriminate between them. Some have obviously been written by the marketing department with little input from those involved in the corporate processes. Guess which will stand the test of scrutiny?

Besides sustainability reports, publicly traded companies in the United States are required to file a form 10-K with the Securities and Exchange Commission. These documents disclose any material risks faced by a company, an illuminating document to review. They are often available on the investor relations page of a company's website.

As you can see, there are a variety of ways to make the business case for sustainability. What is most important is to make the business case relevant to that particular business, to its culture and to its values. Pasting on a business case from another industry will not fly. It must be filled with the language of the internal corporate culture. It must be able to inspire the management team as well as the employees in the office pool or on the factory floor. Once this is accomplished, there will be buy-in across the company and the sustainability program can flourish.

Supplementary Reading Suggestions

Some good books in this area include the following:

- Anderson, R. (2009). *Confessions of a radical industrialist.* New York: St. Martin's Press.
- Esty, D. & Winston, A. (2006). *Green to gold.* New Haven: Yale University Press.
- Humes. E. (2011). *Force of nature: the unlikely story of Walmart's green revolution.* New York: Harper.
- Lazlo, C. (2008). *Sustainable value: how the world's leading companies are doing well by doing good.* Palo Alto: Stanford Business Books.
- Savitz. A.W. & Weber, K. (2006). *The triple bottom line.* San Francisco: Jossey-Bass.

Additional publications of note:

- Global Environmental Management Institute (GEMI). (2001). Value to the top line. Available from: http://www.gemi.org/GEMIPublications.aspx
- Hoisington, S.H. & Menzer, E.C. (May, 2004). Learn to talk money. *Quality Progress* (44-49).
- ISO. (2009). ISO 31000: Risk management — principles and guidelines. Available from: http://www.iso.org/iso/home.htm
- SIGMA Project. (2003). The SIGMA Guidelines; Putting Sustainable Development into Practice – A guide for organisations. Available from: http://www.projectsigma.co.uk/
- SIGMA Project. (2003). The SIGMA guidelines – toolkit; SIGMA business case tool. Available from: http://www.projectsigma.co.uk/

- SIGMA Project. (2003). The SIGMA guidelines – toolkit: SIGMA opportunity and risk guide. Available from: http://www.projectsigma.co.uk/

References

Blackburn, W. (2007). *The sustainability handbook*. Washington, DC: Environmental Law Institute Press.

Confino, J. (2012). Rio+20: Unilever CEO on the need to battle on to save the world. *The Guardian*. Retrieved from: http://www.guardian.co.uk/sustainable-business/rio-20-unilever-battle-save-world?intcmp=239

Ford Motor Co. *An american legend*. as quoted in Blackburn. 2007. P. 104.

ISO. (2009). ISO 31000: Risk management — principles and guidelines. Available from: http://www.iso.org/iso/home.htm

MIT Sloan Management Review & The Boston Consulting Group (MIT & BCG). (2009). *The business of sustainability*. Cambridge, MA: Massachusetts Institute of Technology. Available from: http://sloanreview.mit.edu/special-report/

MIT Sloan Management Review and The Boston Consulting Group (MIT & BCG). (2011). *Sustainability: the 'embracers' seize advantage*. Cambridge, MA: Massachusetts Institute of Technology. Available from: http://sloanreview.mit.edu/special-report/

Porter, M. & Kramer, M. (2011). Creating shared value. *Harvard Business Review*, 89 (1/2).

SIGMA Project. (2003). *Sigma business case tool*. London: The Sigma Project Press.

Waddock, S. & Bodwell, C. (2007). *Total responsibility management: the* manual. Sheffield, UK: Greenleeaf Publishing.

Willard, B. (2009). *The sustainability champion's guidebook; how to transform your company*. Gabriola Island, BC, Canada: New Society

Chapter 4

Sustainability Footprint

Inefficiency is masked because growth and progress are measured in money, and money does not give us information about ecological systems; it only gives information about financial systems.

—*Paul Hawken*

Introduction

Footprint is a bit of a buzzword these days. The global ecological footprint is a popular topic among environmentalists. You may have calculated your own ecological footprint on one of many popular websites. How many "earths" does it take to support your lifestyle? The Global Footprint Network predicts that if every person in the world lived like the average American, it would take five planets to support us all (http://www.footprintnetwork.org). This is certainly an unsustainable trend.

From a corporation's perspective, it is important to understand the word *footprint* in its own context. In this case, we want to create an inventory of the activities, products, and services that are associated with the organization. Then we can calculate what their impacts are on the environment and society.

How much energy, water, and materials are consumed in the production of the company's products or services? This can be a relatively complicated number to calculate, especially if you are including the supply chain as well as all the connecting processes integrated into the organization. (For instance, where does the company get its energy? From a coal-fired power plant or from wind generation?)

Sometimes the location of the organization is important as well. Bottling operations for beer or soda companies are highly water intensive. A bottling operation in a desert region would have different impacts than in a water-rich area. Data centers are intensive energy users and are often located near hydroelectric power plants. Computer companies are locating some of their manufacturing facilities in China due to its virtual monopoly on rare earth minerals.

In addition, the organization needs to consider the effect of its products after they've been purchased by customers. If the company produces cell phones or computers, how much energy is used over the product's lifetime? The same is true for a washer, a refrigerator, or an automobile. If the company produces clothes that must be dry-cleaned, what is the long-term effect on the environment? Or how many times do blue jeans get washed? Some companies are paying attention to these effects and are designing their products to reduce their impacts over an estimated lifetime.

For example, Levi Strauss performed a life cycle analysis of their jeans and found that half of the water used in production is consumed through growing the cotton. Fabric production itself is also water intensive and can involve harmful dyes and chemicals. As such, the company is trying to reduce that impact in partnership with the National Resources Defense Council. Finally, Levi Strauss found that a large portion of their product's resource consumption occurs after consumers take the jeans home. A 50 percent reduction in climate impact could be achieved by washing the jeans in cold water and line drying instead of using a dryer (http://www.levistrauss.com/sustainability/product/life-cycle-jean).

First Things First: Boundary

As you can already guess from the examples provided, it is important to first determine the boundary of the footprint analysis. For many companies, doing so may be a step-by-step process, beginning first within the confines of a particular facility and then, as the analysis progresses, branching out to suppliers, customer use, and secondary supporting facilities, such as distribution channels and power sources.

The analysis can get quite complicated, but that is partly the point. If a company wants to truly understand its impacts and to find ways to manage its resource use, it needs to get down and dirty in the details. As Amory Lovins, co-founder of Rocky Mountain Institute, likes to say, "In God we trust; all others bring data."

Tools for Footprint Analysis

Various tools can be used to develop a sustainability footprint. We will look at a few that are most common, including those that follow:

- Process mapping
- Life cycle analysis
- Activity inventory in the value chain
- Balanced scorecard

Process Mapping

One of the most useful tools for analyzing the sustainable footprint of a company—especially when looking at just a particular facility—is called *process mapping*. A process map is a visual tool that helps a company understand not only its core processes but also its supporting processes and their linkages. Resources and personnel are included as both inputs and outputs. A *process flow* includes all of the related activities that are used in the process from beginning to end.

Figure 4.1 below shows a typical process flow map. In this case, it is read from left to right, but process maps can also be read from top to bottom. The process can be divided into sub-processes that show the relationships between the processes or the hierarchy, as well as lists of resources and personnel used in each step. These lists are called *resource accounting sheets*.

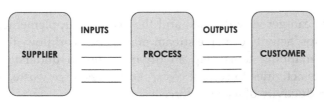

Figure 4.1: Typical Process Flow Map
(Anderson, 2009a)

Mapping all of the processes and supporting processes for an operation can better facilitate the identification of wasted resources and redundancies. Once it is all mapped out on paper, it is easier to see where resources are duplicated or how a process could be modified to make it more efficient. Perhaps materials are stored in a place where they are used by various processes. Would it be better to relocate some of the processes so that they are all close to the materials needed? Or perhaps personnel move from one area to another to facilitate supporting processes. Could either the people or the activities be moved or realigned?

Process mapping includes not just the core processes but also the supporting processes or systems (e.g., air pollution control, water treatment, tool shop, storage room) and infrastructure processes or systems (e.g., HVAC, restrooms, first aid, parking lot). Some of the supporting processes may require their own maps. There are even universal figures and shapes for some of these designs, also referred to as unified modeling language developed by an international standard (Anderson, 2009a). Figure 4.2 shows an example of some of these symbols.

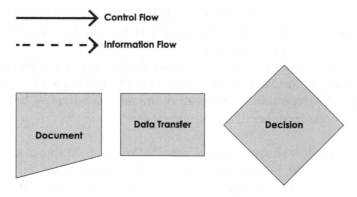

Figure 4.2: Unified Modeling Language Symbols
(Anderson, 2009a)

Process maps can get very detailed and they can be supplemented with document maps, activity or value stream maps, and workflow diagrams. All of these mapping tools help an organization to understand and standardize its activities to control costs, reduce resource waste, and increase the productivity of its work force.

Various software programs facilitate the creation of these maps. Using the maps in training sessions can facilitate communication among the workers and management regarding particular processes. Having pictures helps to "see" the processes more clearly, thereby improving communication. Figure 4.3 below illustrates a typical workflow map containing process phases that can be connected by "swim lanes" to show how responsibilities flow between personnel (Anderson, 2009b).

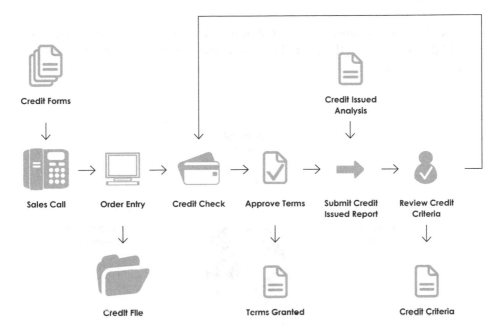

Figure 4.3: Workflow Diagram
(Anderson, 2009b)

Once again, the data and information brought to light through the process mapping exercise is worth the effort. Some are daunted by the detail involved, but teams of people can work on these maps, making the whole exercise more meaningful. With a complete inventory of the resources and activities required for each process, it becomes possible to more clearly identify risks that need to be reduced as well as any opportunities on which the company should capitalize.

Life Cycle Analysis

You are probably familiar with the idea of a *life cycle analysis* or a *life cycle assessment* (LCA). An LCA is a cradle to grave analysis or inventory of all environmental (and hopefully social) impacts generated from the production of a particular item. It includes the extraction of the materials used, manufacturing of the product, packaging and shipping, use of the product, any repair or maintenance, and ultimate reuse, recycling, or disposal.

Figure 4.4 below shows the outline of a typical LCA. As you can see, it is a high-level view of the overall production and ultimate reuse or disposal of a product.

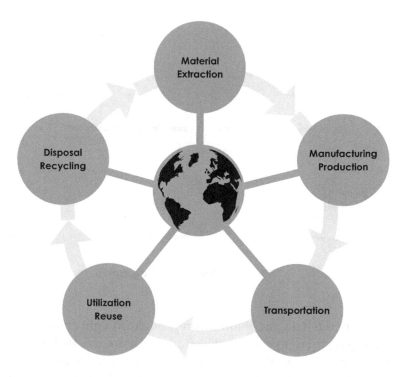

Figure 4.4: Elements of a Typical Life Cycle Assessment
(NIST, 2008-2012)

An LCA can be very useful when determining the basic impacts of a product from both an environmental as well as a social standpoint. The first LCAs were developed in the 1960s and 1970s during the energy crisis. Coca-Cola was one of the first to conduct such an analysis, focusing on the environmental releases and resource consumption of various beverage containers. Since then, LCAs have become much more sophisticated. As a result, companies can find them more difficult to understand and implement.

Any comprehensive LCA necessarily involves volumes of data, and while some companies welcome the detail, others shy away from the challenges that come with communicating the results. As a leading official in the Danish Environmental Protection Agency explained, "We need to find a simple way of communicating the results of LCA because most people have neither the time nor the interest to read entire documents. But if the answers are simple, then...the question of credibility arises—because there is no way for [stakeholders] to check the validity of the results" (EEA, 1997, p. 14).

Still, LCAs are becoming more and more integral to company planning, especially when developing a new product line or preparing for major changes in production or materials. These analyses have evolved to a sophisticated level, incorporating a multitude of data points and weighing the various measurable impacts to form an overarching environmental profile. Even then, value judgments need to be made. For example, when evaluating a laptop computer or a cell phone, how much aluminum, silicon, and copper are contained in a given device? Are there differences between various models? Where were those materials sourced? Were human rights issues involved in the resource extraction?

At the same time, LCAs may require broad assumptions based on the weight assigned to various concerns. Which is more important: water or energy? The answer may differ depending on where the activity occurs. These sorts of necessary assumptions and judgments have put LCAs under some criticism.

Some help can be obtained from an international standard (ISO 14040) that was developed in the late 1990s and was updated in 2006. This standard helps to apply a more universally accepted framework around some of these decisions.

In addition, the "80–20 rule" can be helpful here. Sometimes referred to as the Pareto principle, it states that 80 percent of the problems can be attributed to 20 percent of the causes. In this sense, an LCA can be analyzed to find the sustainability problem areas or "hot spots" such that most of the attention and analysis can then be focused on those areas.

To be most successful, an LCA involves a partnership between those doing the research and those involved in the production itself. Here, a clearer set of priorities and judgments can be made every step of the way, ensuring that potential hot spots are not overlooked and that every essential detail is provided when and where needed (Shepard, 2011).

Value Chain Activity Inventory

A third way to measure the footprint of a company and its products is to consider each step in production as an "activity." Michael Porter of Harvard University introduced the concept of activities and the value chain in his 1985 book *Competitive Advantage*. In it, he explains that every organization is a collection of activities that are combined to implement the production, marketing, delivery, and support of the products it sells. All of these activities are part of the organization's *value chain*. The costs of these activities can be measured and managed (Porter, 1985, p. 36). Figure 4.5 below shows a typical value chain as envisioned by Michael Porter.

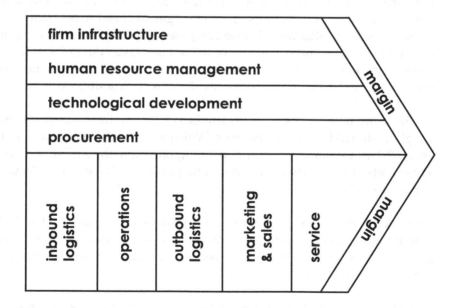

Figure 4.5: The Generic Value Chain (Porter, 1985, p. 37)

Porter describes cost as one of the two types of competitive advantages a firm can possess (the other being differentiation), and he argues that most companies do not have a systematic method for analyzing costs. Developing a framework around the value chain enables a company to better analyze costs. By doing so, Porter argues that a company can better control the costs of a variety of activities (1985, p. 62). This can also be done from the perspective of resources used and resources lost, including the social impacts from each activity.

According to Porter, there are ten main drivers of cost (or drivers of cost savings) in the value chain, as follows (1985, pp. 70-83):

1. Economies of scale
2. Learning
3. Capacity utilization
4. Linkages among activities
5. Interrelationships among business units
6. Degree of vertical integration
7. Timing of market entry
8. Firm's policy of cost or differentiation
9. Geographic location
10. Institutional factors (e.g., regulation, union activity, taxes)

A company can obtain a competitive advantage by reducing costs in these areas over those of its competitors or by reconfiguring their processes in the value chain (think process mapping) in order to reduce costs.

Differentiation is the other type of competitive advantage mentioned by Porter, and in this area, we can begin to see how times have changed since 1985. He speaks mostly of differentiation in terms of quality of materials, as in superior work force training to produce a better quality product or technology advantages (1985, p. 122).

However, since his book was published, Porter has written extensively about the value chain and how it can be affected by a company's response to environmental and social responsibility (for example, in the last chapter, I mentioned Porter's concept of shared value). Creating value through differentiation in the areas of environmental and social responsibility also relate to Porter's concept of buyer value. Consumers and stakeholders today consider these areas important. Hence, paying attention to economic and social impacts can create value for a company.

Determining the Appropriate Footprint

After reviewing the various ways to look at a corporate sustainability footprint, how does one actually determine a specific footprint for a company? First, as was said at the beginning of this chapter, you must determine the boundary of the footprint to be calculated. Sometimes a company will begin with just its manufacturing facility and will eventually expand the footprint to include the supply chain and beyond. Next, it is important to determine the priorities of the particular company and its stakeholders (including its investors and customers). We will go into this in more detail later, but for now, it is sufficient to understand that the core values and vision of the company, as well as the needs and wishes of the company's stakeholders, make up part of the decision.

For example, for a company like FedEx, reducing their transportation footprint became an important priority. FedEx received widespread attention for introducing highly efficient hybrid electric trucks. In addition to saving money, they also gained points in terms of their reputation. Even so, their environmental management director stated, "We understand the business case for doing this. But what sold this inside our company wasn't the business case, but the appeal to our core values" (Googins, 2007, p. 109).

Risk is also an important concern. The challenges may vary from one industry to another. In the energy industry, for instance, risks may include energy security, climate change, or policy changes. In the retail industry, supply chain practices (such as labor practices in foreign suppliers) or consumer issues may rise to the top. For the food and beverage industry, the major concerns may be trade and globalization, health and nutrition, and also climate change (Googins, 2007, p. 99).

Here is where you can start to think about combining techniques. By understanding the inputs and outputs of resources (both human and natural resources) from the process mapping and the LCA, the value chain analysis can help a company determine where the highest costs are for various resources used and lost. This can help to prioritize where to act. Where can the company get the best value? How can resources be conserved with the least cost? What types of human resources can be made more productive? Where are the biggest risks should social problems go unresolved?

The views of various stakeholders can impact the prioritization of these risks as well. A 2005 survey by McKinsey & Company found that the top concerns of customers can vary from those of the business executives (McKinsey, 2005). Hence, communicating with stakeholders and mapping their concerns is a key component of making the sustainability footprint a useful tool.

Balanced Scorecard

Leading sustainability companies are using the tools described in this chapter to develop a *balanced scorecard* to prioritize and rate their own progress along the path to sustainability and to chart their own progress regarding their sustainability footprint. The term *balanced scorecard* refers to the notion that both financial and non-financial information are included in the analysis, using both "leading" and "lagging" indicators. The Latin American firm Amanco, an important producer of plastic piping for fluid transport, served as a case study for a Harvard Business School article in 2008 regarding the value of using a sustainability scorecard to improve business value.

Amanco has received numerous sustainability awards for their work, but their efforts have also increased their market share. Amanco understands that building plastic pipes means more than just manufacturing and selling a product. Several years ago they made serving their stakeholders a priority. They developed compensation systems within the company to improve performance and their reputation, not just to increase profits. This led to the development of a sustainability scorecard that kept track of environmental and social responsibilities as well as monetary value.

By involving their production employees and sales force in the mapping process, they were able to create a robust, customized sustainability footprint for the company. An example of Amanco's sustainability scorecard is shown in the appendix to this chapter. They used the tools described here to develop this illustration, and they used the information provided by their scorecard to increase productivity and expand their markets across Latin America (Kaplan & de Pinho, 2008).

In this way, process mapping can better inform the activities value chain described by Porter; or an LCA can be used to inform some of these activities and to reduce costs. Larger, more sophisticated companies are learning more about these tools and are therefore finding ways to stay ahead of their competition, both in terms of controlling costs and differentiating themselves from their competitors through more responsible production practices.

Supplementary Reading Suggestions

There are a number of short, concise articles on process mapping by Chris Anderson, a leading business process consultant, available on the website Bizmanualz. These articles offer a more through explanation and examples should you be interested in learning more about these tools:

> You can start with the article, "What is a Process Map?" (http://www.bizmanualz.com/blog/what-is-a-process-map.html) and then follow the links at the bottom of that article to a series of additional articles about various types of process maps.

The following article contains a history and analysis of LCA:

> Svoboda, S. (1995). Note on life cycle analysis. National Pollution Prevention Center for Higher Education, University of Michigan

A more comprehensive report was produced by the European Environment Agency, which includes links to many other sources of information:

> European Environment Agency (EEA). (1997). *Life Cycle Assessment: A guide to approaches, experiences, and information sources.* Retrieved from: *www.eea.europa.eu/publications/GH-07-97.../Issue-report-No-6.pdf*

More information on the concept of the balanced scorecard can be found in the following *Harvard Business Review* article:

> Kaplan, R.S. & Norton, D.P (2005). Using the balanced scorecard as a strategic management system. *Harvard Business Review.*

For those interested in alternate media, you can watch a brief video of Professor Kaplan here:

> YouTube video of Robert Kaplan and the Balanced Scorecard: http://www.youtube.com/watch?v=oNy8kupW8oI&feature=related

References

Anderson, C. (2009). What is a process map? *Bizmanualz*. Retrieved from: http://www.bizmanualz.com/blog/what-is-a-process-map.html

Anderson, C. (2009). Seven types of process maps – part III. Retrieved from: http://www.bizmanualz.com/blog/seven-types-of-process-maps-part-iii.html

Googins, B., Mirvis, P, & Rochlin, S. (2007). *Beyond good company; next generation corporate citizenship*. New York: Palgrave MacMillan.

International Finance Corporation (IFC) & SustainAbility. (2007). *Market movers: lessons from a frontier of innovation*. Washington, DC & London: International Finance Corporation & SustainAbility.

Kaplin, R.S. & de Pinho, R. R. (2008). Amanco: developing the sustainability scorecard. *Harvard Business School*.

NIST. (2008-2012). Sustainable manufacturing program. Retrieved from: http://www.nist.gov/el/msid/lifecycle/sustainable_mfg.cfm

Porter, M. (1985). *Competitive advantage: creating and sustaining superior performance*. New York: Simon and Schuster.

Shepard, D. (2011) Uncovering sustainability opportunities in your product line. Sustainserv. Retrieved from: http://www.sustainserv.com/easyblog/entry/uncovering-sustainability-opportunities-in-your-product-line.html

University of Bolton. (2012). Concepts of printed circuit design. Retrieved from: http://www.ami.ac.uk/courses/ami4809_pcd/unit_02/

Valarde, Israel. (2007). Case: Amanco for a better Peru. Asia Pacific Economic Cooperation.

Appendix: Balanced Scorecard

Amanco Group's Sustainability Scorecard
(Adapted from Allard, I., p. 20 and IFC & SustainAbility, 2007, p. 41)

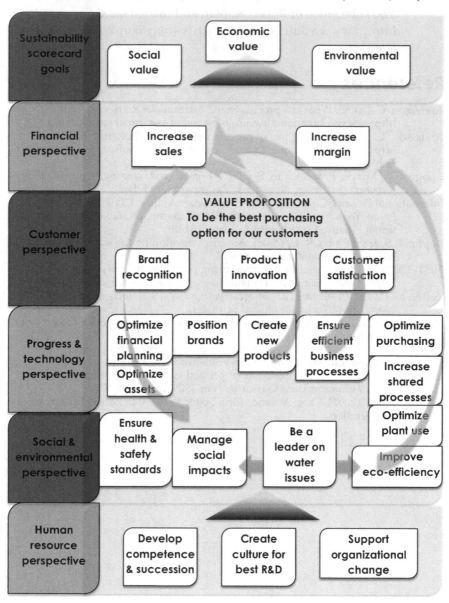

Chapter 5

Governance and Management

If management is about running the business, governance is about seeing that it is run properly.

—Robert I. Tricker

Introduction

Robert Tricker is widely known as the father of corporate governance having authored a book by that title in 1984. In it, Tricker defined *corporate governance* as follows (1984, p. 6):

> The governance role is not concerned with the running of the company, per se, but with giving overall direction to the enterprise, with overseeing and controlling the executive actions of management, and with satisfying legitimate expectations of accountability and regulation by interests beyond the corporate boundaries.

Although this definition does not specifically imply checks and balances with respect to corporate responsibility toward society and the environment, modern scholars include these as part of corporate governance. Internal and external checks and balances are needed to ensure that nothing is overlooked, as well as to ensure that emphasis is placed on accountability and transparency toward stakeholders (Solomon, 2010).

Basic Corporate Structure

Corporate structure varies around the globe. Not all companies are structured in the way that they are in the United States or in northern Europe. In Russia and China, for example, state control has a heavy influence on how corporations are governed. In the Middle East, religious beliefs and family ownership play a prevalent part. And in Southeast Asia, local legal and cultural factors are influential (Solomon, 2010).

For our purposes, we will focus on the Anglo-Saxon model prominent in the Unites States. Today's US corporations operate under state statutory law rather than being chartered by individual governments, as was the case for the East India Company mentioned in Chapter 2. Corporations have many of the same rights as individuals—they can own property, pay taxes, sue, and be sued.

As a result of a Supreme Court ruling in 1886, a corporation is considered a "natural person" under the US Constitution and is therefore free to lobby legislators, establish educational institutions and charitable organizations to further their interests, and to use mass media to project the image they wish to present to the general public, all in the interest of "free speech" (Robbins, 1999). And, thanks to a more recent US Supreme Court ruling, they also have the same First Amendment right of free speech regarding the use of their resources to influence political elections (Liptak, 2010).

Corporations have an unlimited lifetime and a separate identity from the people who create them. They function through their agents, officers, and directors, and they continue to exist in spite of the change in identity of these individuals. Although they do not have an expiration date, corporations can be terminated through dissolution, bankruptcy, merger, or other actions.

Ownership of a corporation is held by its stockholders or shareholders. They receive dividends as declared by the board of directors and these dividends are paid based on the number and type of shares of stock they own in the company. Large corporations often have both common stock, which usually includes voting rights of one vote per share, and preferred stock, which is usually considered nonvoting, but which includes preference in dividend payments as its name implies. The shareholders vote to elect the corporation's board of directors, and in large corporations, this is usually done by proxy, which is a legal document allowing an individual to appoint another individual to act on their behalf (Pride, 2010, p. 118).

Limited Liability

One of the most important aspects of a corporation is its limitation on liability. With few exceptions, shareholders in a corporation are not personally liable for the acts of the corporation. A corporation can own property, but it does so in its own right. It therefore exists separately from its shareholders. Although a corporation can sue or be sued, its liability is thus limited to the extent of its assets. Any claim for damages does not pass through to its shareholders, directors, or other officers (Pride, 2010, p. 120).

This limitation on liability from legal claims against individuals does not, however, protect a corporation from a damaged reputation. More and more, corporations today see the risks involved in merely complying with regulations and therefore not creating real value for their shareholders through responsible management policies. That is part of why sustainability has become such a buzzword in today's business world.

Bylaws and Articles

Corporations are regulated by statute, but they also adopt their own articles of incorporation and bylaws. The articles control the basic structure of the corporation, such as the number of directors and the voting of shares. The bylaws establish the day-to-day operations of the business, such as policies on negotiating contracts, hiring employees, and disbursing funds.

The state where the articles of incorporation are filed controls the domicile of the corporation and in that state the corporation is a *domestic corporation*. In all other states where that corporation does business, it is considered a *foreign corporation*. The corporation must therefore register in all those states and pay annual fees and taxes. Corporations incorporated outside of the United States are called *alien corporations* (Pride, 2010, p. 117).

Board Members and Responsibilities

The two major responsibilities of a corporation's board are to oversee the long-term strategic direction of the company and to hire, evaluate, and set compensation levels for top management. The board is also ultimately responsible to the corporation's shareholders, creditors, employees, customers, and suppliers, and is also responsible for complying with legal and regulatory requirements, including environmental and social responsibilities.

Many boards (especially at smaller and more regional companies) are largely comprised of people from the company's management structure. Any outside members may have little traction or lack enough information to disagree with management recommendations or to question the company's traditions. This can cause a company to fall behind changes in market demands. Walter Salmon argues in a Harvard Business Review book (2000, pp. 3-5) that corporate boards should have no more than three insiders on the board—the chief executive officer (CEO), the chief operating officer (COO), and the chief financial officer (CFO) or the "C-Suite"—and that most public companies should be comprised of eight to fifteen members.

Who determines who will serve on the board? Although half of the companies listed on the New York Stock Exchange have nominating committees, it is somewhat surprising to learn that a survey by Korn/Ferry found that almost 90 percent of them depend on the recommendations of the chairman (often the CEO) for new members. What does this do to the culture of an organization? Does this encourage objective oversight of the company or does it endanger a company to pack its board with people unlikely to question the CEO's decisions?

Consultants, lawyers, bankers, and suppliers to the company should possibly be disqualified from board service (Salmon, 2000, p. 10). Finally, board diversity—including race, background, and gender—are obviously an asset for any corporation.

Figure 5.1 below shows an overall view of board responsibilities and how they relate to the activities performed by a corporation. Conformance to standards and accountability to stakeholders is in one quadrant, which is focused more on results (actions that have already happened). Performance, including policies and strategies, relate more to future plans.

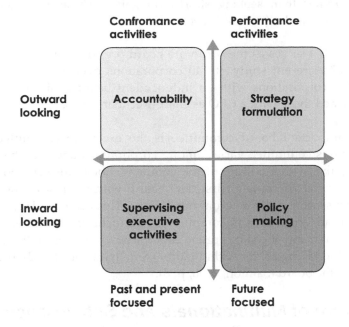

Figure 5.1: Inward versus Outward Focus of the Board
(Tricker, 2012, p. 45)

Board Committees

Two important board committees are the audit committee and the compensation committee. The audit committee is charged with overseeing the annual independent audit of the company's financial statements and ensuring that regulations and accepted financial principles are followed. Some suggest that audit committees could have more responsibility, including the oversight of high-risk areas within the company to ensure that appropriate reserves are maintained in order to protect the company from loss (Salmon, 2000, p. 6).

The compensation committee sets the compensation for top management, including salary, stock options, and identifies formulas to determine short-term and long-term incentives. Consultants are often hired to advise board committees. The comparables used to determine salary levels are usually pulled from similar corporations in the same industry, often those of competitors. Should the compensation committee be given more power? Should they look outside the industry for comparables to ensure long-term vision and accountability of top management rather than seeking short-term gains? These are interesting questions to consider (Salmon, 2000, p. 7).

Often the CEO serves as the corporate board president or chair. Is this a good idea? A recent study of 140 corporations over a six-year period found that corporations with an independent board chair consistently outperformed those with a CEO as chair (Rechner, 1991).

Another important board committee is the executive committee. The power of this committee varies among corporations and may be determined by the overall culture of the company. Some are very powerful and can in effect become a "first tier" board, with the rest of the board merely consenting to their recommendations. This can be a danger. Given current advancements in communication, including the Internet and video conferencing, it can be argued that the executive committee should be limited to taking action within parameters that have already been approved by the board (Salmon, 2000, p. 8).

Structure of Multinationals and Subsidiaries

The basic structure of a multinational corporation typically includes a corporate headquarters in one country with facilities in various other countries. There are three basic variations on this structure:

1. The most common model includes a corporate headquarters, which is located in one country, with various production facilities operated in other countries where the cost of production is lower due to labor prices or resource availability.
2. As an alternative, the parent company may be based in one country with relatively independent subsidiaries located in other countries. In this case, most of the operations functions are housed in the parent company, but subsidiaries are opened in other countries with just a few basic ties to the parent company.
3. Using a third approach, the parent company oversees a diverse conglomeration of subsidiaries in various countries that may even include different industries. This would result in a looser grouping of affiliates and subsidiaries with only some operations that are more directly controlled by the parent company.

In these examples, the parent company refers to the portion that owns or controls more than 50 percent of the subsidiary companies' stock. A subsidiary is a company that is owned or controlled by another company.

Subsidiaries have their own boards and their own missions, and they may belong to an entirely different industry than the parent company. However, since the parent company holds a controlling interest, the parent company can control who sits on the board and therefore who is hired to manage the company.

A corporation may have a number of affiliates, wherein the ownership of stock is a minority interest rather than a controlling interest. Two companies may also be affiliates if they are both owned by one parent company.

Organizational Culture

Organizational culture can have a profound impact on how a corporation operates, who is chosen for key positions, and how it approaches its economic, environmental, and social responsibilities. An organization's culture can outlive its products, founders, and leadership, acting as a backdrop to any strategy implemented by the organization.

Culture can operate at various levels in an organization, including:

- The first level includes the more obvious attributes: the physical facilities, furnishings, dress code, and visible awards and recognition symbols, as well as human interactions within the company
- The second level includes the "declared" culture: vision and mission statements, company slogans, and expressed values within the organization
- The third level is less obvious, more intuitive, may not surface from company interviews and surveys, and may reflect in the organization outwardly expressing values of one type when in actuality the organization behaves quite differently

Understanding these three levels of organizational culture can help to explain how some companies can become dysfunctional.

Global companies often wrestle with cultural issues when they establish subsidiaries and production facilities in other countries. Ensuring that these diverse units adapt to the overall corporate culture is an important part of management practice. For example, in some countries, the local values for human life can impact attitudes toward safety and the environment (Ionescu-Sommers, 2008, pp. 151-153).

Vision, Mission, and Core Values

So far, mission, vision, and core values have come up quite a few times in this book. So what do these terms really mean and how important is it for a company to clarify these ideas? And what do they have to do with sustainability?

The *vision* of an organization summarizes its long-term goals. The vision should resonate with all parties involved. Uplifting in nature, a company's vision should also serve to broaden the views and capabilities of its members, providing the framework or direction toward which all strategies and plans are formulated.

The vision statement for Interface, a leader in sustainable manufacturing of carpeting and other institutional interiors, reflects their overall goal (http://www.interfaceglobal.com/Company/Mission-Vision.aspx):

> To be the first company that, by its deeds, shows the entire industrial world what sustainability is in all its dimensions: People, process, product, place, and profits—by 2020—and in doing so we will become restorative through the power of influence.

A *mission statement* is a statement of ongoing objectives and priorities for an organization. It should summarize the essence of the vision and goals, and ideally, it should be a statement that any employee can remember and repeat. Some companies get a bit carried away, producing mission statements of a paragraph or more. The following is PepsiCo's mission statement. This is an example of one that would be hard to memorize. (http://www.pepsico.com/Company/Our-Mission-and-Vision.html):

> Our mission is to be the world's premier consumer products company focused on convenient foods and beverages. We seek to produce financial rewards to investors as we provide opportunities for growth and enrichment to our employees, our business partners, and the communities in which we operate. And in everything we do, we strive for honesty, fairness, and integrity.

Internally, mission and vision statements help to guide and inspire both management and the employees at all levels. They help to formulate strategies and ensure ethical behavior. Externally, these statements can serve as a way to inform customers and the general public about the overall goals of a company while also creating accountability for those goals (Heathfield, 2011).

There is often debate about whether a company should modify its vision or mission statement following the decision to improve its sustainability efforts. Should the vision include a specific charge toward environmental, social, and economic responsibilities? Or do the current mission and vision imply this goal? Regardless of the answer, it is a healthy debate for any organization.

For a company like Patagonia, a leader in both environmental and social responsibility, their mission statement clearly reflects these values (http://www.patagonia.com/us/patagonia.go?assetid=2047):

> Build the best product, cause no unnecessary harm, use business to inspire, and implement solutions to the environmental crisis.

Guiding Principles (Core Values)

One way to link sustainability to a vision or mission statement that would otherwise be difficult to change is through core values. Many companies list their core values along with their mission and vision. Incorporating environmental, social, and economic values into this list can be a way to connect sustainability to a company's overall mission and vision.

Core values should be developed through vigorous discussion within an organization. Sometimes they originate from a company founder and are handed down through generations; they may therefore require updates or modification. Core values should reflect management's overall approach and should guide the behavior of everyone in the company. Hiring and promotion policies can be influenced by these values. They may also impact overall goals and priorities.

Many companies publish their core values in their annual reports and on their websites. Some, like Whole Foods, create signage in their retail establishments for all to see. Listed below are the core values held by Whole Foods. Note that they include all three areas of sustainability—environmental, social, and economic—and that they also mention the importance of suppliers as well as the local community. These statements employ a positive and energetic tone, presenting clear and inclusive messages. These therefore represent a good example for any company to consider because they may spur discussion of other creative ideas (http://www.wholefoodsmarket.com/company/corevalues.php):

- Selling the highest quality natural and organic products available
- Satisfying and delighting our customers
- Supporting team member happiness and excellence
- Creating wealth through profits and growth
- Caring about our communities and our environment
- Creating ongoing win–win partnerships with our suppliers
- Promoting the health of our stakeholders through healthy eating education

The board is usually involved at the higher levels of an organization with respect to the company's vision and mission. The board may also help to set the core values. But management and the employees implement this vision, so it is important that they embrace not only the mission but also the company's core values. Figure 5.2 below helps to illustrate how this would operate from a management perspective.

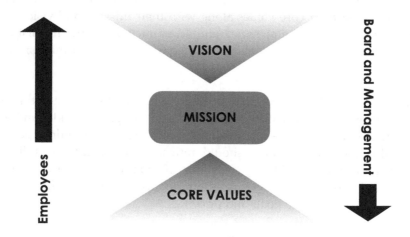

Figure 5.2: Implementation of Vision, Mission, and Core Values

Ultimately, every aspect of a company—from company policies to personal conduct to stakeholder engagement—should reflect the values that are promulgated. Making them public helps to ensure that both internal and external stakeholders are reminded of these values on a regular basis; stakeholders will therefore be more likely to uphold them.

Does a company need a sustainability policy as such? If they are using an integrated management system such as ISO 14001 (environmental management) or ISO 9001 (quality management), they will be required to do so. Many companies leading the charge in sustainability have incorporated sustainability into their overall vision and mission in addition to creating a separate sustainability policy. Most companies that are serious about sustainability adopt a sustainability strategy or plan, which includes specific goals and a timeline.

Unilever, a widely recognized leader in sustainability, has adopted a Sustainable Living Plan with a clear strategy to imbed sustainability into its business at all levels and to measure and report on their progress. Unilever has created a team of "sustainability champions" throughout the company to ensure that their commitment continues. They have even linked compensation to sustainability goals for the CEO and other top managers (Unilever, 2011).

Empowering Employees

Management and the board of any company are certainly responsible for the overall performance of a business, but that responsibility also falls to every employee in the company. Corporations are beginning to recognize that no matter how much time is spent creating policies and frameworks, if the employees on the floor or in the field are not engaged, then much effort has been wasted.

Many companies employ systems to solicit and process feedback in order to encourage employee participation. Toyota has become a leader in employee feedback through its continuous improvement program referred to as Kaizen. Employees are asked to suggest incremental and ongoing improvements. Involving the employees in decision making promotes personal responsibility and a sense of ownership. Motivation is therefore increased and productivity is improved.

Who resists their own idea? Isn't it better to come up with your own improvement idea versus being told how to improve? These are key concepts with respect to unleashing the potential of a work force and overcoming stubborn resistance to change. Sustainability thrives on ingenuity and fresh perspective. Empowering the work force with a sense of confidence makes sustainability more accessible (Doppelt, 2003).

Guidelines and Standards

There are a number of international guidelines and standards to help ensure that corporations are governed properly with the appropriate balance and oversight to ensure a healthy and successful operation. The Australian Standard AS 8000-2003, *Good Governance Principles*, provides specific guidelines regarding the role, powers, and responsibilities of the board, as well as suggestions regarding board education, committees, and equitable treatment of shareholders. It stipulates, for example, that the board is responsible for setting the strategic direction of the company; approving budgets; reviewing performance; ensuring compliance with legal requirements; ensuring that risks are identified and managed properly; fostering a culture that fits the company's values and vision; appointing the CEO; and evaluating the CEO's performance (Standards Australia, 2003a, p. 14).

Adopted in 2003, the Australian Standard for organizational codes of conduct (AS-8002) outlines how to draft such a document, including how to comply with applicable laws, maintain the organization's integrity while avoiding conflicts of interest, and provide aspirational goals for the organization (Standards Australia, 2003b).

The Global Reporting Initiative (GRI) guidelines are less prescriptive. Still, they offer good guidance regarding corporate governance through the process of asking a corporation to analyze its own practices and thereby suggest the best actions. In section four of the GRI guidelines, for example, corporations are asked whether the chair of the board is also the CEO as well as how many independent members serve on the board (GRI, 2000-2011, pp. 22-23).

In the United States, the Sarbanes-Oxley Act of 2002 (SOX) also applies to larger corporations. Enacted partially in response to the scandals of WorldCom and Enron, this law applies primarily to the financial management and transparency of financial controls. Section 404 of the act requires management and auditors to report annually on the adequacy and scope of internal controls over financial reporting (http://www.soxlaw.com/s404.htm). While SOX applies specifically to companies doing business in the United States, there are similar laws in other countries. If all companies followed the standards mentioned in this section, more than likely the need for SOX would not have arisen.

B Corporations

A number of alternative corporate structures have appeared on the horizon offering new possibilities for sustainability. There are several varieties, but one that appears to be gaining ground is called the *B Corporation*. B Corporations follow a slightly different legal structure for a corporation, one that has been accepted in about half a dozen states in the United States. It involves a higher set of standards that require the business to address the environmental and social concerns of sustainability. Companies who agree to these standards are protected from sale to investors who do not agree with the standards adopted as part of the corporate structure.

Companies are certified through B Lab, a nonprofit organization organized to formulate the guidelines. B Lab appoints an independent standards advisory council, which oversees the certification ratings and auditing for B Corporations.

This is a new area in sustainability to watch. Will B Lab be the appropriate overseer for this new corporate structure or should a more diverse group of stakeholders be involved in the process? It is early in the game, but this new structure may bode well for sustainability in business. To find out more about B Corporations, go to the B Lab website: http://www.bcorporation.net. Figure 5.3 below shows the logo attributed to B Corporations. Watch for it. As of 2013, over 700 companies were designated B Corporations.

Figure 5.3: B Corporation Logo

Conclusion

Governance systems for modern corporations pursuing sustainability have evolved, striving to develop and implement a whole systems approach to management. Management systems are employed as a means to drive sustainability into daily operations, involving employees at all levels. Such systems foster innovation and creativity making companies more nimble and more responsive to market needs while also providing brand strength through responsible behavior.

Conversely, companies with a more traditional vertical hierarchy tend to create a series of sustainability initiatives, putting sustainability into separate silos within the company. As a result, these programs often die from lack of attention or an inability to justify their existence (Doppelt, 2003).

The implementation of a comprehensive management system is a continuing theme for success in the sustainability field. It has become a widespread practice among those companies who excel at supporting internal feedback systems that solicit ideas for growth and improvement. Empowering employees at all levels of the company to come forward with suggestions and innovation is critical to successful governance. Companies who are leading the sustainability charge have incorporated these systems into the very fabric of their operations.

Supplementary Reading Suggestions

The Sustainability Reporting Guidelines developed by GRI provide a comprehensive framework for sustainability reporting. GRI is a nonprofit organization that includes a global network of experts who contributed to formulation of this framework and participate in its governance. The most recent version of the GRI guidelines, version 3.1, is available for free download on the GRI website. As this book went to press, a new version G4 was being released.

Part 1 of the 3.1 guidelines describe what to report and how to define the boundaries of the report. Part 2 describes the basic content of each of the types of areas to report, including economic, environmental, and social responsibilities, and specifically outlining areas of human rights, labor practices, and product responsibility. Pages 22 and 23 of Part 1 specifically focus on governance.

See the GRI website for more information and to download the guidelines:
https://www.globalreporting.org/reporting/guidelines-online/G31Online/Pages/default.aspx

Additional resources are available from various nonprofit global governance organizations. Two leading organizations are as follows:

- Global Corporate Governance Forum (part of the International Finance Corporation): http://www.gcgf.org/
- International Corporate Governance Network (ICGN): https://www.icgn.org/

The Center for Corporate Citizenship at Boston College has published an excellent white paper that outlines the benefits of vision and values for modern corporations. It describes how aligning these concepts with stakeholder values can promote company success. The paper further emphasizes the importance of minimizing harm, maximizing benefit, being responsive to key stakeholders, and supporting strong financial results. See:

Rochlin, S.A. & Googins, B. K. (2005). *The value proposition for corporate citizenship.* Chestnut Hill, MA: The Center for Corporate Citizenship at Boston College. Available from: www.bc.edu/corporatecitizenship

References

Doppelt, B. (2003). *Leading change toward sustainability.* Sheffield, UK: Greenleaf Publishers.

Freeman, E. R. (2001). A stakeholder approach to strategic management. In M. A. Hitt, *Handbook of Strategic Management* (p. 189). Maden, MA: Blackwell Publishers, Ltc.

Global Reporting Initiative (GRI). (2000-2011). *RG; Sustainability reporting guidelines, version 3.1.* Amsterdam: Global Reporting Initiative.

Ionescu-Sommers, A. & Steger, U. (2008). *Business logic for sustainability.* New York: Palgrave Macmillan.

Liptak, A. (2010, January 21). *Justices, 5-4, Reject corporate spending limit.* Retrieved July 12, 2010 from The New York Times: http://www.nytimes.com/2010/01/22/us/politics/22scotus.html

Perlmutter, H. V. (1993). The tortuous evolution of the multinational corporation. In G. &. Hedlund (Ed.), *Organization of Transnational Corporations* (pp. 295-299). New York: Routledge.

Pride, W. H. (2010). *Business.* Mason, OH: South-Western Cengage Learning.

Rechner, P. L. (1991). CEO duality and organizational performance: a longitudinal analysis. *Strategic Management Journal*, 12 (2), 155-160.

Robbins, R. (1999). *Global problems and the culture of capitalism.* Allyn and Bacon.

Salmon, W. J. & Lorsch, J. W. (2000). *Harvard Business Review on Corporate Governance.* Boston: Harvard Business School Press.

Solomon, J. (2010). *Corporate governance and accountability.* Wiley & Sons.

Standards Australia. (2003a). *AS 8000 – 2003.* Sydney: Standards Australia International.

Standards Australia. (2003b). *AS 8002 – 2003.* Sydney: Standards Australia International.

Tricker, B. (1984). *Corporate governance: principles, policies and practices.* New York: Oxford University Press.

Tricker, B. (2012). *Corporate governance: principles, policies and practices, second edition.* New York: Oxford University Press.

Unilever. (2011). *Unilever sustainable living plan; progress report 2011.* London: Unilever PLC

Chapter 6

Stakeholder Engagement

If we are listening to the dialogue, if we are open to learning from each other, we are probably going to make better decisions as a company.
—Dan Henkle, Gap, Inc.

Introduction

A well-run company with a clear vision and strong core values, strong monitoring systems, and a balanced set of metrics has a good chance of succeeding in today's world. But that same company may miss key markets, fall behind its competitors, or even ignore important risks that could devastate its reputation should it fail to listen to and actively engage with its stakeholders.

In his best seller *Good to Great*, author James Collins emphasizes that great companies are able to confront "the brutal facts" (Collins, 2001). This means having the courage to listen to important stakeholders but also to ask for their viewpoints and to reflect these viewpoints into decisions made concerning products and services. Stakeholder insight can provide valuable lessons. Their insight may not only reduce risk and the likelihood of boycotts, lawsuits, or production delays, but it may also provide clues to future demand. For example, what types of products would their customers want in the future? In this sense, stakeholder engagement can help businesses move from a strategy of risk management to a more advanced and integrated strategic management for competitive success.

Stakeholder engagement involves more than just paying lip service to survey results. Rather, it includes participating in meaningful discussions, entering into problem-solving analyses, and undertaking planning processes together. And it's more than just working with customers and suppliers. Stakeholder engagement should include NGOs, activists, government officials, joint venture partners, and employees (Blackburn, 2007, p. 373).

In this chapter, we'll take a look at some of the principles of stakeholder engagement, including how to drive a successful engagement program. We will also try to understand the pitfalls and discuss how best to avoid them. There are some excellent stakeholder engagement guides that provide more detail and guidance. Various international standards also offer information to help identify the most important issues.

Prioritizing Stakeholders

Stakeholders include a multitude of individuals and groups, any and all of whom can affect a company's activities. They include the obvious examples—investors, employees, customers, and suppliers—but they also include the local community, the media, NGOs, competitors, labor unions, and regulatory agencies.

Certain stakeholders may be more important depending on the particular issue being addressed. Some may have alliances that grow or change depending on the emphasis or perspective at hand. Mapping the various stakeholders and their priorities can be a complicated maze. For that reason, many companies emphasize the importance of building trust and maintaining open communication with stakeholders rather than trying to follow specific maps or charts (SRA, 2005, p. 12).

Regardless, certain stakeholder groups will remain of primary importance, while others will tend to remain more peripheral. Figure 6.1 below shows a typical arrangement of stakeholders according to priority.

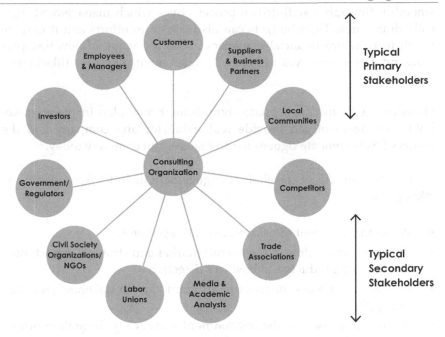

Figure 6.1: Typical Primary and Secondary Stakeholders
(SRA, 2005, p.12)

Engaging with these stakeholders can take a variety of forms, including the following (SRA, 2005, p. 14):

- Educational opportunities, such as employee training, brochures for customers, websites, or reports;
- Consultation, including focus groups, surveys, and workplace assessments;
- Dialogue, including seminars and forums, advisory panels, and leadership summits; and
- Partnerships, including alliances, joint ventures, and public–private partnerships.

Analyzing the interests of stakeholders and actually engaging with them can be daunting for some companies. Even though doing so seems beneficial in principle, human nature may intervene. The engagement process can be a bit of a bumpy road, with challenges popping up from unexpected or even openly hostile groups. The exchange can also create uncertainty, complicating decisions that would otherwise progress smoothly through a staff-driven process over which management typically dominates. Tight budgets can also constrain efforts and it may be tough to convince financial managers about the value of devoting precious time and resources to "cushy" engagement measures (Blackburn, 2007).

However, with the appropriate commitment and plan in place, stakeholder engagement can provide real value for any company and the process has become de rigueur for any successful company today.

Some of the benefits of stakeholder engagement include (AccountAbility, 2005, p. 9):

- Better management of risk and overall reputation
- Better understanding of the overall market and strategic opportunities for new products and business direction
- Product and process improvements learned from stakeholders such as suppliers
- Improved impacts on the environment and society through informing and influencing other stakeholders
- More equitable management based upon input from important stakeholders and influencing decisions
- Building trust with stakeholders
- Pooling resources beyond the confines of the company to resolve technical, social, environmental, or economic problems

Stakeholder engagement can be encouraged by raising awareness within the company and among company managers regarding its many benefits; by providing access to training and tools available for engagement; and finally, by making it a clear goal for the company and rewarding those managers who pursue stakeholder engagement (Blackburn, 2007).

Performance Framework Perspective

Performance frameworks or performance management systems are used by a variety of organizations to drive excellence and to measure performance against objectives and strategies. Many such systems are employed around the world, some of which are industry-specific. One excellent framework is the Baldrige Criteria for Performance Excellence, which is managed by the National Institute of Standards and Technology

(NIST), an agency of the US Department of Commerce (Baldrige, 2011-2012).

The Baldrige Criteria are typical of many performance frameworks and the supporting document emphasizes the importance of stakeholder engagement, especially from the perspective of the company itself and its customers. A link to the Baldrige Criteria is provided in the supplementary reading section at the end of this chapter, but we'll take a look at some of the most important concepts here in terms of how they relate to stakeholder engagement.

Leaders

The Baldrige Criteria consider leadership to be an important component for driving performance excellence. The leaders of an organization are responsible for formulating and communicating the company's vision and core values throughout the company as well as among its stakeholders. At the same time, the direction set by corporate leadership should balance the value and interests of all stakeholders while providing an environment that allows for action and innovation based upon those needs.

Success in any organization is dependent on the ability to continually improve and innovate. A company must be able to anticipate the direction required, a result that comes through successful stakeholder engagement organized by the management of the company. This engagement also requires the empowerment of employees at all levels of the company in order to ensure the implementation of stakeholder engagement, which means providing opportunities for learning and for soliciting and ingesting feedback from the work force. The ability to act on ideas from both within and outside of the company provides the kind of agility that can keep a company ahead of its competitors, therefore providing long-term viability (Baldrige, 2011-2012, p. 36).

Within the leadership category, the Baldrige Criteria emphasize the importance of governance and social responsibility of the organization. By requiring a transparent and accountable governing structure, the organization can more successfully realize its public responsibilities and maintain its license to operate. Leaders are encouraged to work within the governance system in order to behave legally and ethically and to promote the practice of good citizenship throughout the organization.

To encourage organizations to have fruitful and productive conversations about leadership, the Baldrige Criteria ask a number of questions rather than stipulating specific standards. This helps businesses to customize their management systems in order to better perform in particular markets and circumstances (2011-2012, p. 7).

Leaders and Governance

The Baldrige Criteria also ask how an organization uses its governance system to address responsibilities to the public, to ensure ethical behavior, and to practice good citizenship. Specifically, the Baldrige Criteria pose the following question (2011-2012, p. 8):

> How does your organization review and achieve the following key aspects of your governance system?

- Accountability for management's actions
- Fiscal accountability
- Transparency in operations as well as selection and disclosure policies for governance board members
- Independence in internal and external audits
- Protection of stakeholder and stockholder interests, as appropriate

This section goes on to ask questions about how performance reviews are conducted for senior leaders as well as the governing board. In addition, the criteria ask how these evaluations are used to improve both personal performance as well as the effectiveness of the governing system.

The Baldrige Criteria emphasize legal and ethical behavior from the perspective of fulfilling social responsibilities as well as supporting key communities. Once again, this reinforces the importance of any organization's license to operate in the communities in which it is located.

The questions here focus on how an organization investigates the ways in which its activities impact society. How are they evaluated and how are they addressed? These questions also relate to stakeholder engagement. For example, how can an organization anticipate future concerns of the public? How can an organization be proactive rather than reactive? How could a particular organization conserve the use of natural resources, including those required in its supply chain? In addition to asking about key regulations and measures necessary for compliance with those regulations, the criteria ask how the organization is structuring its processes and implementing goals to surpass those requirements—to go beyond compliance. Finally, this section of the criteria asks how these goals and processes are addressing the most important risks associated with the organization's activities (Baldrige, 2011-2012, p. 8).

These are ideas that we've been discussing; here we're looking at those concepts from the perspective of stakeholders. The Baldrige Criteria recognize this perspective as crucial and pose direct questions concerning how governance and leadership address stakeholder concerns and how they interact with stakeholders and "key communities" to do so. The criteria also ask how the organization is monitoring and responding to these concerns.

Asking these sorts of questions forces the organization to structure its planning and management system around these important ideas. Further, it helps to drive sustainability into the company's organizational systems.

Employees

The Baldrige Criteria also recognize employees as an important area of focus with respect to performance. They use the term *work force* rather than *employees*. This category focuses on helping an organization to assess its ability to build an effective and highly performing work force. This includes both the capabilities of the employees as well as creating the right environment in which to produce a high-quality product or service. The criteria ask questions about how the organization hires, organizes, and manages its employees in alignment with its own mission, vision, and core values. This includes engaging with personnel in meaningful ways to encourage their own goals and desires and to encourage a diverse culture of ideas and perspectives (Baldrige, 2011-2012, p. 18).

This section includes two principle questions (pp. 18-19):

1. How do you build an effective and supportive work force environment?
2. How do you engage your work force to achieve organizational and personal success?

Topics that relate to the first question—building an effective and supportive work force environment—include compensation and support of career growth as well as how the organization's work processes enable its employees to perform in the best possible manner. Once again, the Baldrige Criteria don't specify how to accomplish this task. Rather, the criteria include a number of questions through which a company can rate itself (2011-2012, p. 18).

Companies may have a variety of needs in order to develop its work force, depending on the size and scope of the operation and the organization's stage of development. The questions posed here help an organization to focus on what is important now as well as what areas should be considered for future planning. Employee development is a fluid operation. The planning and implementation cycles build on each other year after year in order to provide continuous improvement and innovation.

Customers and Other Stakeholders

As any business owner knows, the customer is a very important stakeholder for any organization. Listening to and learning from the customer base and involving them in product and service decisions will help any business become more sustainable. Interaction with customers should go beyond marketing and sales. Ideas for new products and services can often come from customers. Listening to their ideas can not only help to resolve issues of concern but can also improve customer loyalty and lead to business expansion. Sometimes, customers have a false view of the business and its operations. Listening to customers can help organizations to improve their communication techniques, ultimately allowing the company to reach other customers as well.

The Baldrige Criteria focus on customers from two perspectives: first, *listening* to the customer to obtain important feedback about products or services, and second, *engaging* with customers to build relationships and increase market share (2011-2012, pp 13-14).

The first perspective, listening, relates to obtaining information on customer satisfaction, both good and bad. This type of information can help an organization to better understand its marketing and branding, and it may enable an organization to design products that the customer wants. This information also drives innovation and branding, and it can even drive important decisions concerning resource use and work force treatment. What kinds of risks is the company taking by using resources that are obtained through mining in developing countries where laws are lax and workers are treated poorly? What kinds of risks are taken by companies that depend on manufacturing facilities in countries where labor laws allow for child labor or long hours for little pay? These and other questions are important for a business to evaluate as they may help to eradicate a risk before it becomes an issue that might seriously damage the organization's brand and image (Baldrige, 2011-2012, p. 13).

The second perspective, engagement, refers to developing relationships with key customers or groups of customers in ways that will improve marketing and enhance customer loyalty. Engagement drives innovation as a result of the information gathered. It can help to build a more "customer-focused culture" for the organization. This can even lead to a kind of root–cause analysis for the organization, helping to identify the real cause of customer complaints and then to eliminate those issues through process improvement (Baldrige, 2011-2012, p. 40).

Supply Chain

The Baldrige Criteria address supply chain engagement through questions regarding the company's work process management. Ensuring that suppliers provide quality and reliable products that meet customer satisfaction and performance requirements is key to managing the company's work processes (Baldrige, 2011-2012, p. 22).

Together with the customers, suppliers are involved in the life cycle of the process, product, or service. Many companies engage with suppliers through collaborative meetings or conferences. Supplier codes of conduct are becoming more prevalent in the sustainability supply chain as companies become more concerned about the treatment of employees in supplier factories and about environmental damage in the acquisition of various resources.

External Stakeholders

The Baldrige Criteria and other performance frameworks focus mostly on internal performance; they are not focused on external stakeholders other than customers. But external stakeholders can have an enormous impact on a corporation, especially one that operates in a global marketplace.

Communities

The community in which a company operates can have an enormous impact on the performance of a company. Factors include an organization's ability to hire quality employees, gain access to community services like improved transportation systems or expanded facilities, taxation and regulation, and even the general community atmosphere for those employed at the facility. This is all part of the "license to operate" in a community. More and more, companies are engaging proactively to ensure that necessary services are available and that neighborhood concerns are addressed before they spiral out of control.

Companies like Shell and Intel have formed facilitated advisory panels in the communities in which they operate. These panels handle concerns related to noise, pollution, traffic, or emergency preparedness. Other companies such as Alcoa hold local meetings in addition to open houses and tours. Many organizations publish sustainability reports to educate their constituency. Some even rely on surveys to collect relevant input (Blackburn, 2007).

Governments

Engagement with governmental agencies can take a variety of forms, from lobbying legislators to working with local regulators on special projects or permits. Organizations such as the International Council for Local Environmental Initiatives (with over twelve hundred local government members) and Ceres (which works with investors and companies as well as policy makers) help to provide leadership and to promote dialogue between governments and business. These types of organizations as well as other NGOs can provide a valuable resource for business stakeholder engagement.

NGOs

The number and influence of NGOs has increased dramatically over the past several decades. Actual numbers are difficult to determine as the NGO status embraces a multitude of organizations including labor unions, foundations, and religious organizations. But it is well accepted that NGOs have grown in prominence and influence in recent years.

Why should a company engage with NGOs? The simple answer is that given their power and influence, NGOs have a bully pulpit of sorts that enables them to have a significant impact on a business and its license to operate, not only in its local community but also with its customer base. NGOs also have more credibility than corporations or even governments according to many surveys. This gives them enormous power to sway public opinion and influence a brand's image (Blackburn, 2007).

How should a company engage with NGOs? There are a number of approaches suggested by William Blackburn (2007, p. 411):

- *Rub elbows:* Participate in groups where NGOs are involved. Join Ceres, for example, and attend their conferences or participate in the GRI guideline review process. This enables personal communication and allows you to gain insight into what motivates the NGO and to seek out common ground.
- *Conduct an NGO impact assessment:* Larger companies perform detailed analyses of various NGO groups operating in their sectors and update these lists on a regular basis. Understanding their goals and targets can help to avoid unpleasant surprises.
- *Evaluate NGO fit:* Selecting an NGO for engagement involves not only finding the overlap between the NGO's focus and the company's actions but also determining whether the NGO's profile fits the overall scope of the company engagement. Local issues may require more care and attention. You may not want to deal with an international NGO on certain localized problems unless that NGO has a particular local focus. Verifying this fit will enable more successful engagement.
- *Manage company expectations:* Sometimes it's simply not possible to reach an overall agreement. It is therefore important to manage expectations with respect to the engagement process. Patience and understanding will pay off when it's not possible to agree on all points.

Overall, NGOs are a growing force in the world of sustainability, and if approached in a positive manner, they can provide support and will be of benefit to the engagement process.

Tools for Engagement

Okay, so we've assembled our shopping list of those stakeholders who we need to approach and engage. How do we go about doing that without tripping over ourselves?

There are a number of well-vetted tools available to companies wanting to enact a successful stakeholder engagement program. AccountAbility has published a stakeholder engagement standard, AA1000, as well as two comprehensive manuals on stakeholder engagement. The AA1000 standard, first published in 2005, was revised in 2011 in response to a pilot study of the original plus discussions with various stakeholder groups from twenty different countries. As stated in the introduction to the standard, stakeholder engagement often results from a company responding to a crisis and then realizing that engagement can be more than just "pain alleviation." It can lead to real value and operational excellence (AccountAbility, 2011, p 8).

The standard outlines a three-step process for stakeholder engagement (AccountAbility, 2011):

1. *Commitment and integration:* First, the organization needs to commit to the three accountability principles of AA1000 AccountAbility Standard (2008), which are: inclusivity, materiality, and responsiveness. *Inclusivity* means engaging stakeholders at all levels, making sure to include them in the decision-making process. *Materiality* means finding the most relevant and important issues for stakeholders (and realizing that some issues may be more important for different stakeholders). *Responsiveness* includes the alternatives chosen, actions taken, performance, and communication that pertain to the material issues. Further, this commitment needs to be *integrated* into the governance and strategic management of the company—to become part of how the company is managed on a day-to-day basis, not just a separate program to be reported on and placed in a separate silo (pp. 12-14).

2. *Purpose, scope, and stakeholders:* Next, the company needs to establish its own *purpose* for stakeholder engagement. Why are they doing this? The most common reasons are as part of an overall strategy or to improve operations, but these reasons should be linked specifically to the company and to the company's activities. The *scope* of the engagement also needs to be defined. What is the subject matter? What divisions of the company will be included? What is the time frame? And finally, the *stakeholders* need to be defined. Who will be included in the process of engagement? As the process is defined, adjustments may be made based on input from the various parties (pp. 16-18).

3. *Stakeholder engagement process:* Third, the company should prepare an appropriate process to ensure successful implementation. This is similar to the familiar plan-do-check-act process that is defined in other standards, such as the more common ISO 14001 environmental management standard. But here, AccountAbility uses the terms *plan, prepare, implement,* and *act-review-improve.* First, the company should prepare an overall *plan* by profiling and mapping the stakeholders. Next, it should *prepare* by mobilizing the appropriate resources and building capacity within the company for the implementation. *Implementation* includes inviting the appropriate stakeholders to participate and documenting the results of the engagement. Finally, *act-review-improve* includes monitoring and evaluating the progress, making adjustments, recommending future actions to improve the process, and, of course, reporting on the appropriate recommendations for changes in company strategy or procedures as a result of the engagement process (pp. 22-43).

In addition to the AccountAbility standard, there are two comprehensive manuals that were created by AccountAbility in partnership with two other organizations. These organizations offered input influenced by interviews with a wide variety of companies, NGOs, labor unions, and other stakeholder groups. These two publications—*The Stakeholder Engagement Manual,* volume 1 and volume 2—are included in the supplementary reading section and are available from the AccountAbility website for free download. Anyone organizing a stakeholder engagement program would benefit from a deep dive into these volumes as they include sample forms and charts for use in the process of engagement as well as suggestions for planning and implementation.

In particular, volume 2 goes into the planning process in a bit more detail and divides the three steps above into more stages. Figure 6.2 below shows how they put these pieces together. You can see that the ideas presented are basically the same as those presented in the AA1000 standard, but the manual goes into more detail by providing step-by-step processes to guide the company.

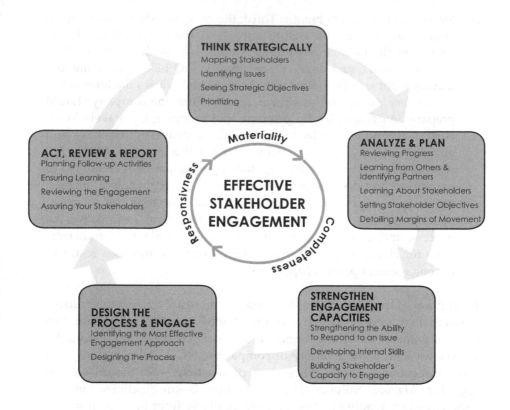

Figure 6.2: Stakeholder Engagement Process
(Accountability, 2005, p. 11)

The point to emphasize is to think strategically before beginning the process. Spend some time early on evaluating how the strategic business objectives relate to stakeholder interest. Consider how to prioritize those stakeholders based on the strategy of the company. Then planning can begin incorporating different levels of engagement, from education to partnerships. Help the organization learn more about the process before taking action.

Strengthening capacities for engagement in the organization and making sure that the necessary resources are available are crucial considerations before beginning the actual engagement. If you don't have the right staff ready and trained with any other necessary resources available, the whole process could come to a screeching halt or worse—it could end in embarrassment. Once the plan and framework are ready, the actual engagement process can begin, moving through the various stages, progressing until results are obtained.

Finally, the act, review, and report stage provides a focused analysis and review of what went well and what could be improved, such that future engagement can be better managed and problems avoided (AccountAbility, 2005, p. 10).

Concluding Thoughts

Many suggested formats for engaging stakeholders exist, but most include this basic approach: first, think about who your stakeholders are, map them out accordingly, and then put together a strategy and a plan for engagement. Make sure you have adequate resources devoted to the effort before you begin and then design the process. Engage with a variety of stakeholder groups, carefully recording your results and reviewing them for appropriate action. Put together your recommendations for change and make sure to review any necessary adjustments or modifications. Then begin again, this time using the knowledge you acquired in the first round. Successful stakeholder engagement is a continuous process of improvement.

Supplementary Reading Suggestions

An excellent sustainability guide, *The Stakeholder Engagement Manual*, volume 1 and volume 2, was produced by a joint venture between AccountAbility, referenced previously; Stakeholder Research Associates, a Canadian firm that combines academic research and consultancy focused on stakeholder engagement; and UNEP, which provides leadership and encourages partnerships between governments and other organizations to promote social and environmental responsibility. These volumes are excellent for anyone seeking a framework for sustainability engagement.

- Volume 1 provides a summary of interviews with corporations, NGOs, labor unions, and trade organizations regarding the importance of and value received from stakeholder engagement.

- Volume 2 provides concrete suggestions regarding how to implement a stakeholder engagement program, including sample charts and forms to use in the process.

The AA1000SES (2011) Stakeholder Engagement Standard produced by AccountAbility is also a valuable tool and provides the general framework to guide a sustainability program.

All three of these publications are available for free download from the AccountAbility website:

> http://www.accountability.org/about-us/publications/index.html.

The Baldrige National Quality Program's *Criteria for Performance Excellence* is updated every couple of years. The most recent version is available for purchase from the NIST website:

> http://www.nist.gov/baldrige/publications/business_nonprofit_criteria.cfm.

Earlier versions of the Baldridge Criteria can be found easily on the Internet, and they would provide a helpful guideline for any company considering using these guidelines.

References

Baldrige National Quality Program (Baldrige). (2011-2012), *2011-2012 criteria for performance excellence.* National Institute of Standards and Technology (NIST). Retrieved from: http://www.nist.gov/baldrige/publications/business_nonprofit_criteria.cfm

Blackburn, W. (2007). *The sustainability handbook.* Washington, DC: Environmental Law Institute Press.

Collins, J.C. (2001). *Good to great: why some companies take the lead;... and others don't.* New York: HarperCollins.

Stakeholder Research Associates Canada, Inc. ("SRA"). (2005). *The stakeholder engagement manual, volume 1: the guide to practitioners' perspectives on stakeholder engagement.* Cobourg, Ontario: Stakeholder Research Associates Canada Inc., United Nations Environment Programme, AccountAbility.

AccountAbility. (2005). *The stakeholder engagement manual, volume 2: the practitioner's handbook on stakeholder engagement.* London: AccountAbility, the United Nations Environment Programme, and Stakeholder Research Associates.

AccountAbility. (2011). *AA1000SES (2011) stakeholder engagement standard, final exposure draft.* London: AccountAbility.

Chapter 7

Environmental Stewardship

I stood indicted as a plunderer, a destroyer of the earth, a thief of my grandchildren's future. And I thought, my God, someday what I do will be illegal. Someday they'll send people like me to jail.
                                                            —*Ray C. Anderson*

Introduction

Ray Anderson is no longer with us, having passed away in 2011 after a battle with prostate cancer. But his legacy lives on and his leadership in the environmental field is universally acknowledged. Fortunately for us, Ray wrote a book about his experiences, *Confessions of a Radical Industrialist*, which is a terrific read as well as an inspiration to other industry leaders (Anderson, 2009).

It wasn't always that way for Ray, however. As explained in his book, Anderson founded Interface Inc., a carpet company, in 1973. For twenty years, he built a profitable and "responsible" company from his point of view. Interface met all of the legal environmental and social requirements. But in 1994, Anderson had an epiphany that changed his life, changed the direction of the company, and raised the bar for production excellence in his industry and beyond.

Ray explains that a memo appeared on his desk in 1994 from a sales associate on the West Coast, which stated that customers were inquiring about what Interface was doing for the environment. "How should we answer?" asked the associate. This concept wasn't exactly news to Ray, but the question spurred an examination that led him to Paul Hawken's book, *The Ecology of Commerce* (published in 1995). In it, Anderson found a story that set him off.

The story was about the reindeer of St. Matthew Island, a tiny island off the coast of Alaska used by the US Coast Guard during World War II. A rough and craggy place to say the least, the island had been stocked with reindeer as a hedge against starvation should the troops become stranded. This scenario worked well until the Coast Guard abandoned the site after the war, leaving the reindeer to graze comfortably on lichen and willows with not a predator in sight.

By 1963, the original population of twenty-nine reindeer had ballooned to six thousand. The formerly fat and happy group had munched the lichen to stubs; hardly a twig remained. Three years later when a biologist visited again, there were only forty-two left alive as the others had succumbed to starvation. It was a classic case of overshooting and it became a "spear in the chest" moment for Ray Anderson (Anderson, 2009, p. 13).

Hawken connected this scenario to the role of business in society. Humans and our industrialization, he argued, had caused the decline of living systems across the globe—species approaching extinction, resources in decline, pollution mounting. The linear system of take, use, and throw away the by-product was mounting to a level that could no longer be sustained. Hawken predicted that we were headed toward a doomed future of overshoot unless we radically changed the way that we produce goods and consume resources.

But Hawken's message wasn't all doom and gloom. Although business and industry were the main cause of the problem, Hawken argued they were also the only entities with enough size, wealth, power, and influence to resolve the problem. Neither government nor religious organizations nor NGOs could solve the issue. Rather, businesses represented our one hope.

Anderson's fire was lit. He realized that he needed to make a big change in the way he led Interface. To do so, he made a personal commitment to make his organization a global leader in environmental responsibility, going beyond the regulations, setting an ultimate goal of zero waste, using only resources that could be regenerated, while remaining profitable in the process (Anderson, 2009, pp. 9-17).

The journey of Interface carpet is still in process and continues beyond Ray Anderson's leadership. As a company, they have made enormous progress toward those goals and have proven that it is possible to be both environmentally and socially responsible while also profitable. In this chapter, we will investigate some of the tools used by Ray Anderson and Interface to meet their environmental goals, as well as those used by other industry leaders around the world.

Natural Capitalism

In addition to writing *The Ecology of Commerce*, Paul Hawken wrote another book with Amory and Hunter Lovins, a book that has become a foundation for the sustainability field. *Natural Capitalism*, published in 1999, outlines the earth's various resources from the perspective of capital assets and earned income. This is the basic principle of any economist: use just the income earned off of the principal asset; don't spend the asset itself. If you use up your assets, you cannot sustain your existence. Period.

The concept of natural capitalism divides the world's resources into four basic areas (Hawken, Lovins, & Lovins, 1999, p. 4):

- Natural capital: natural resources, living services, and ecosystems
- Human capital: human labor and intelligence, culture, and organization
- Manufactured capital: machines, tools, factories, and infrastructure
- Financial capital: cash, investments, and monetary instruments

In this chapter, we will focus on natural capital, the environmental resource that needs to be protected and renewed to provide for a sustainable existence. In the next two chapters we will consider human capital (social well-being) and then financial and manufactured capital (economic prosperity).

The argument made by the authors in *Natural Capitalism* is that the supply of natural capital is not unlimited. Humankind has reached a point where its impact on the earth's ecosystems is in danger of "overshooting," to use Paul Hawken's term. The remedy, the authors argue, is to move away from the traditional capital economy of continuous growth and use of resources to a *service and flow* economy, in which society is provided with the services it needs rather than more products.

For example, an elevator company would sell the *service* of its elevators, providing the lifting and lowering of its customers, while maintaining ownership and responsibility for repair and replacement of the elevator itself. This encourages the production of a higher quality product using recycled materials, rather than a throwaway product, the parts and materials for which are simply replaced.

Four central strategies enable the switch to a more resource-respectful system (Hawkins, Lovins, & Lovins, 1999, p. 10):

1. *Radical resource productivity:* This results in a three-pronged benefit: lowering the depletion of resources, decreasing the amount of waste, and providing meaningful employment worldwide.
2. *Biomimicry:* By imitating the way nature uses and recycles resources, industrial systems can be designed as closed-loop systems to eliminate waste and toxic chemicals.
3. *Service and flow economy:* This involves a fundamental shift in the relationship between consumer and producer, with an emphasis on quality of service rather than acquisition (and disposal) of goods.
4. *Investment in natural capital:* Reversing the worldwide trend of resource depletion, investment in restoring and expanding stocks of natural capital will allow the biosphere to heal, thereby supporting a future industry of service and flow.

Since the writing of this book, many scholars and industrialists, including Ray Anderson, have followed its guidance. Interface carpet was founded on the concept of leasing carpet squares to companies and replacing the worn squares when necessary. They have since developed the technology to reclaim materials from manufactured carpet and to recycle them into new carpet while also reducing the amount of factory waste. Subaru advertises zero landfill factories in the United States. Walmart is pushing conservation of energy and reduction of waste through its supply chain. Anderson's dream is becoming a reality, but there is still much work to be done.

Environmental "Responsibility"

It is difficult to concentrate on just one aspect of sustainability as the parts and pieces really do overlap. Protecting the environment has social as well as economic benefits, but for the most part, this chapter will focus on the environmental aspects of sustainability. The idea of "responsibility" is also something we will emphasize. This coincides with the notion that responsible management includes not only meeting minimum regulations, as Ray Anderson noted, but going beyond those rules and guidelines to encompass a vision for a better world, one in which resources are renewed and waste is no longer thrown away but is reused or prevented altogether.

This kind of environmental stewardship has been supported by various commissions and groups around the world, organizations that have adopted guiding principles and goals. Two of the most notable are the Earth Charter and United Nations Global Compact.

The Earth Charter Initiative adopted the Earth Charter in 2000 after a global consultation process involving leading environmental and social organizations, businesses, and governmental leaders. The charter has been endorsed by over two thousand organizations worldwide, including the United Nations Educational, Scientific, and Cultural Organization (UNESCO) and the International Union for Conservation of Nature. Its principles apply to all aspects of sustainability, including ecology, society, governmental fairness, and economic justice. Its principles under ecological integrity are as follows (Earth Charter Initiative, 2000):

5. Protect and restore the integrity of Earth's ecological systems, with special concern for biological diversity and the natural processes that sustain life.
6. Prevent harm as the best method of environmental protection and, when knowledge is limited, apply a precautionary approach.
7. Adopt patterns of production, consumption, and reproduction that safeguard Earth's regenerative capacities, human rights, and community well-being.
8. Advance the study of ecological sustainability and promote the open exchange and wide application of the knowledge acquired.

The United Nations Global Compact is a strategic alliance of businesses worldwide, which was formed in 1999 by the UN. Today, it includes over 8,700 corporate participants from over 130 countries. Their overall objective is to "mainstream" ten principles in businesses worldwide and to encourage the support of broader UN goals, including the United Nations Millennium Development Goals.

The organization's ten principles were derived from several universally accepted human rights and environmental documents, including the Rio Declaration on Environment and Development. Originally, there were nine principles, but a tenth was adopted in 2004 to address anti-corruption and bribery. The three principles under environment include (UN Global Compact):

- Principle 7: Businesses should support a precautionary approach to environmental challenges;
- Principle 8: Undertake initiatives to promote greater environmental responsibility; and
- Principle 9: Encourage the development and diffusion of environmentally friendly technologies.

You can begin to see the similarity of themes in these goals. But how should a business implement these principles? This is where other organizations have come into play, providing a framework for businesses to follow in order to make these goals a part of their everyday operations.

Environmental Codes, Indicators, and Standards

As we have seen, a number of environmental codes have been developed that outline environmental responsibility. Before a worldwide effort to adopt such principles was in play, another US organization had begun to develop its own list of codes and guidelines. The Coalition for Environmentally Responsible Economies (Ceres) was founded in Boston in 1988. Its codes, originally titled the Valdez Principles in response to the Exxon Valdez oil spill in 1989, are referred to as the Ceres Principles (http://www.ceres.org/about-us/our-history/ceres-principles).

The Ceres Principles focused primarily on corporate environmental responsibilities, including sustainable use of natural resources, energy conservation, protection of ecosystems, and transparency. Disclosure and dialogue with stakeholders are required, and companies must also publicly report their progress and provide annual assessments regarding implementation.

In March of 2010 Ceres published a more comprehensive guide to incorporate its principles. They drafted an overall planning document that companies could use "to embed sustainability from the boardroom to the copy room" (Moffat, 2010, p. 15). This guide is referenced at the end of this chapter and can be downloaded from the Ceres website at no cost.

Ceres helped to spearhead the development of GRI, the Global Reporting Initiative, which has since taken on the task of reporting criteria. Today, Ceres reviews and critiques the sustainability reports of its endorsers (Blackburn, 2007, p. 658).

GRI is now a leading, global organization headquartered in Amsterdam. Their vision was to include more than just environmental concerns within the reporting framework, incorporating social, economic, and governance issues. Publication of its most recent set of guidelines was generated from the input of over three thousand experts from around the world, including businesses, civil leaders, and labor representatives. GRI has formed coalitions with UNEP and the United Nations Global Compact. In March of 2011, GRI published, version 3.1, which incorporates gender and human rights performance (GRI).

The GRI guidelines include "indicators" for measurement in each area of concern. The environmental indicators include measuring the use of materials, energy, water, effect on biodiversity, and emissions, both effluent and waste. The guidelines also address measuring the impact of products and services, compliance with regulations, and transport (including employee transport), as well as overall impact on the environment. Here are a few examples of environmental indicators from the GRI guidelines (GRI, 2000-2011):

Environment Performance Indicators (pp. 28-29)

EN2   Percentage of materials used that are recycled input materials.

EN5   Energy saved due to conservation and efficiency improvements.

EN10   Percentage and total volume of water recycled and reused.

EN14   Strategies, current actions, and future plans for managing impacts on biodiversity.

EN18   Initiatives to reduce greenhouse gas emissions and reductions achieved.

EN23   Total number and volume of significant spills.

EN26   Initiatives to mitigate environmental impacts of products and services, and extent of impact mitigation.

EN29   Significant environmental impacts of transporting products and other goods and materials used for the organization's operations, and transporting members of the work force.

EN30   Total environmental protection expenditures and investments by type.

A complete listing can be found on the GRI website, which is referenced in the supplementary reading section at the end of this chapter.

As Peter Drucker said, "what gets measured gets managed," and this is part of the power of the GRI guidelines. They present a framework around which an organization can set its own goals. Using the indicators listed, the organization is able to report on their progress toward those goals. The use of a clear, globally recognized set of guidelines also provides an opportunity for a company to benchmark its own performance against the performance of others, and to track its own progress over time (GRI, 2000-2011, p. 3).

As mentioned previously, ISO is another organization currently working in the area of indicators. ISO 14001, probably their best-known standard, describes an environmental management system intended to continually improve the environmental performance of a company. By certifying to this standard, a company outlines its own environmental policy and then develops a plan, implements and operates according to that plan, checks its progress, makes corrective action, and finally performs a management review for future planning and action (i.e., continuous improvement).

Third-party certification to ISO 14001 is often required by customers of a company. This may seem strange at first blush, but if a customer wants to ensure that its supplier is following stringent standards, it may require that supplier to become certified in an area of its concern. This approach is commonly used in the auto industry to ensure quality and environmental responsibility. One challenge of the ISO 14001 standard, however, is that companies set their own goals. For that reason, improvement is not standardized or benchmarked. Even existing violations of environmental regulations are permitted as long as there exists a clear "commitment to comply" (Blackburn, 2007, pp. 688-689).

Even so, ISO 14001 is one of the leading standards followed by industries around the world today. It has encouraged businesses to act more responsibly and has provided valuable tools with which companies are able to implement better production practices and continual improvement. ISO's plan-do-check-act overview is widely accepted as a valuable framework for any SMS. In Chapter 11 the SMS will be more closely examined as a way to mainstream sustainability into the everyday business operations of a company.

Other Sustainability Indicators

Maureen Hart has written extensively on the need for clear and traceable sustainability indicators. She has made several thoughtful observations about how individual indicators for various impacts—such as the amount of carbon dioxide emitted or the amount of toxic chemicals used—must be expanded upon in order to understand the connections between these measurements and their effects on society.

Hart argues that a good indicator should help a company to see a problem before it gets too big to act upon. A good indicator should also help to show what types of action could be taken to resolve the issue. Showing where links between society, the environment, and the economy are weak could show how those links might be strengthened. For example, jobs can affect the poverty rate in a community as well as the crime rate. Clean air and water can impact the health of a community. The need to purify the water costs the local economy. Measuring GDP alone can be misleading as well as it doesn't truly reflect the health of a community or a nation. A natural disaster such as Hurricane Katrina can spur a lot of growth for the cost of repairs, but it doesn't necessarily mean that the area affected is better off (Hart, 1998-2010).

Hart has suggested an alternative approach to linking various indicators specifically in the area of the environment. She suggests connecting the measurement of pollutants and emissions to how they affect the general welfare of the community. The table below is taken from her website:

Table 7.1: Environmental Indicators and Sustainability
(http://www.sustainablemeasures.com/node/90)

Environmental Indicators		
Traditional Indicators	**Sustainability Indicators**	**Emphasis of Sustainability Indicators**
Ambient levels of pollution in air and water	Use and generation of toxic materials (both in production and by end user) Vehicle miles traveled	Measuring activities causing pollution
Tons of solid waste generated	Percent of products produced that are durable, repairable, or readily recyclable or compostable	Conservative and cyclical use of materials
Cost of fuel	Total energy used from all sources Ratio of renewable energy used at renewable rate compared to nonrenewable energy	Use of resources at sustainable rate

Moving toward a set of indicators that truly reflect the benefit to society and the world would help industry to better understand the negative (and positive) impacts of that indicator. The Index of Sustainable Economic Welfare is one such measurement system. It accounts for the negative impacts of some economic activity, such as depletion of resources, and adds to GDP for positive impacts such as unpaid domestic welfare (Hart, 1998-2010).

Regulatory Standards versus Market Approach

Many in the business world argue for market-driven improvements versus regulation. It is very tempting to jump on the market bandwagon as the markets can be a more efficient driver of change and there are significant associated benefits. However, how to strike a balance between a free market economy and a regulated one is a discussion that could keep us busy here for quite some time. Where does that balance lie? With so many companies leading the charge for sustainability, it is encouraging to see that we are making progress. Still, there will always be laggards who need regulation to keep them from destroying the world for the rest of us.

One area that does deserve attention is that of market-driven pollution controls, wherein an overall pollution level can be set and the decision regarding who reduces their individual pollution levels can then be driven by market trades. For example, if the goal is to reduce overall air pollution in a city and there are a number of different industries contributing to the pollution levels, it may be more expensive for one industry to reduce pollution than another (because of particular processes, the age of the factory, geographic location, and so forth). In one example given by Robert Crandall (2008, p. 4) from a study in St. Louis, the cost of reducing particulate pollution for a paper products company was four dollars per ton. In comparison, the cost of reducing particulate pollution for a beer company was $600 per ton. By using tradable permits, the brewery could pay the paper company to reduce the same amount of pollution, benefitting both companies and reducing the overall cost to the local economy.

This is analogous to the approach taken by the EPA to reduce pollution from coal-fired electric plants in its efforts to prevent acid rain. The EPA began the Clean Air Markets program in 1994 and received great acclaim for its success. Many scholars argue that a similar program could be used to reduce carbon dioxide emissions around the world.

Emphasizing Process Improvement

Process mapping has already been emphasized as a valuable tool for understanding how a business is operated and how to find ways to reduce resource loss. Improving processes to increase productivity, reduce energy use, and reduce waste has been widely recognized as a more profitable way to improve environmental impacts. Rather than trying to chase down and fix problems, identifying where problems may occur and preventing them by designing around them or improving operating procedures is a much more efficient approach.

Part of the energy behind the environmental movement has been incited by environmental disasters such as the Exxon Valdez spill. Dana Meadows wrote several articles about this spill. In one, written about a year after the disaster, she noted lessons learned (Meadows, 1990):

Anyone who is concerned about the environment must see that, while it is certainly true that oil companies can and should be more careful, and that much stronger incentives, regulations, liabilities, and enforcements are necessary, the real lesson that leaps forth here is:

IT'S IMPOSSIBLE TO HANDLE OIL WITHOUT SPILLING SOME OF IT.

Even if industry got ten times better at handling oil neatly—which is unlikely—the annual spill would still total one hundred million gallons or the equivalent of ten Exxon Valdez's per year. From that realization follows another:

IF THERE'S ANY PLACE YOU WANT TO KEEP FREE FROM OIL, YOU'D BETTER KEEP OIL AWAY FROM IT ALTOGETHER.

This is good advice and is consistent with the notion presented thus far regarding the use of processes to analyze how business systems can be improved. When a company is handling hazardous chemicals, the risk of a spill or toxic discharge always exists. It is therefore important to consider how to improve the processes in order to avoid the use of dangerous chemicals altogether and to therefore avoid environmental damage.

The EPA's Design for the Environment program encourages partnerships with businesses, environmental groups, and academia to design safer products, reduce toxicity, and find alternatives for chemicals in a range of products. Program members have helped to define best practices in areas ranging from auto refinishing to nail salons. They also offer a labeling certification program to enhance consumer knowledge in this area (http://www.epa.gov/oppt/dfe/).

The Design for the Environment program complements the regulatory power of the EPA by encouraging businesses to reduce their risk of harm to the environment by preventing problems from occurring in the first place. The EPA can provide technical expertise, modeling, and toxicology to help industries find safer alternatives to chemicals that are of a concern to environmental health.

Using LCA can also be useful with respect to business process improvement. Understanding where the largest amount of water or energy loss occurs can help to pinpoint areas where processes can be improved and resource loss reduced. Clothing companies have found that much of the water intensity for their products comes after the clothes are purchased by a customer. Reducing the need for washing by using fabrics that are less prone to odor retention or that repel dirt can reduce water intensity during the product's useful life.

Finally, understanding the impacts of the supply chain for each product is ultimately important as well. Going back to the clothing example, fabrics made and dyed in foreign countries may not be controlled by appropriate regulations. This can be a risk to a producer. What if your customers discover that toxic dyes from production of the fabric are endangering children in a poor country? Is that your fault? Well, it could certainly be conceived as such.

Walmart has made strides in the area of supply chains through its "fifteen questions" campaign for suppliers. The endeavor has received mixed reviews from Walmart's suppliers, but ultimately their approach is having a positive effect on their supply chain, reducing energy use, shrinking packaging materials and waste, and increasing resource efficiency. A link to Walmart's fifteen questions is included at the end of this chapter.

SIGMA Guidelines

Project SIGMA was mentioned in Chapter 2 in reference to their Business Case Tool. SIGMA also has published an excellent guideline for businesses seeking to incorporate sustainability into their practices. The guideline emphasizes overall performance, helping businesses to develop their own goals and measure performance progress including stakeholder engagement and a balanced scorecard.

SIGMA looks at capital from the same perspective as *Natural Capitalism*, though the organization divides human capital into both human and social capital. As a result, SIGMA considers five divisions of capital versus four, but the approach is basically the same: encouraging conservation of capital resources while maintaining and enhancing natural capital.

The SIGMA guidelines are available for free download from the SIGMA Project website. The guidelines are a terrific resource and provide examples as well as suggested additional resources for businesses seeking help.

SIGMA also publishes a number of tools and resources to support stakeholder engagement, such as those related to evaluating risk and opportunity, GRI reporting, marketing, and, of particular relevance to this chapter, accounting for environmental impacts of a company (http://www.projectsigma.co.uk/Toolkit/default.asp).

Concluding Thoughts

Improving the environmental impacts of an industry can be achieved in a number of ways, but ultimately the best route is to improve processes and to design toward minimizing resource use and loss. The principles described in this chapter will help a company to formulate a vision. The various indicators and tools will help to measure a company's progress toward that vision. Ultimately, an SMS can be developed using tools such as ISO 14001 to guide the company along its path toward sustainability. To do so requires commitment and it also requires the devotion and participation of employees throughout the company.

Engaging various stakeholders is an important step in this process. Learning from those both inside and outside of the company can help to determine the most important environmental impacts and risks faced by the corporation. These discussions can also reveal how to prevent those impacts from affecting the profitability of the business. By exploring the various challenges and building consensus between stakeholder groups, a company can anticipate potential problem areas and pursue designs and processes to prevent those problems from occurring.

This takes vision, planning, and a commitment to excellence. The rewards are great for those companies who pursue this path. It is a learning process, but there are excellent tools available to make that goal obtainable, and there are many partners to help along the way.

Supplementary Reading Suggestions

The 2010 Ceres publication, *The 21st Century Corporation: The Ceres Roadmap for Sustainability,* is highly recommended as an integrated and well-presented plan through which a business can incorporate environmental and social concerns into its everyday operations. The publication can be downloaded from the Ceres website at this link:

> http://www.ceres.org/resources/reports/ceres-roadmap-to-sustainability-2010/view.

GRI was formed in 1997 through an alliance between Ceres and the Tellus Institute. The reporting guidelines published by GRI represent the result of multi-stakeholder participation including individuals and organizations from around the world. The version of GRI reporting referenced in this book is version G3.1 published in 2011. As this book went to press, a more recent version was released, version G4, which places more emphasis on materiality of reporting information. More information about the new GRI G4 guidelines can be found at their website:

> https://www.globalreporting.org/reporting/g4/Pages/default.aspx

ISO publishes a number of standards applicable to various areas of business. Their numbering system ensures compatibility across various languages and cultures. Developed by technical committees that span the globe and distributed for public comment before finalization, ISO standards are widely used by businesses worldwide. ISO 14001 (*Environmental Management Systems*) and other standards can be purchased and downloaded from the ISO website:

> http://www.iso.org/iso/home.html.

Information on Walmart's sustainable product index and fifteen questions for suppliers can be found here:

> http://news.walmart.com/news-archive/2009/07/16/walmart-announces-sustainable-product-index.

The SIGMA Guidelines and other SIGMA Project publications are highly recommended as background reading and as a source for useful guidelines and tools. They are available for free download at:
http://www.projectsigma.co.uk/default.asp.

References

Anderson, R.C. (2009). *Confessions of a radical industrialist: profits, people, purpose – doing business by respecting the earth.* New York: St. Martin's Press.
Crandall, R.W. (2008). Pollution Controls. *Library of economics and liberty.*
Retrieved from:
http://www.econlib.org/library/Enc/PollutionControls.html

Earth Charter Initiative. (2000). The earth charter. Retrieved from
    http://www.earthcharterinaction.org/content/pages/Read-the-
    Charter.html

Global Reporting Initiative (GRI). (n.d.) What is GRI? Retrieved September 14, 2012
    from: https://www.globalreporting.org/information/about-gri/what-
    is-GRI/Pages/default.aspx

Global Reporting Initiative (GRI). (2000-2011). *RG, sustainability reporting guide-
    lines, version 3.1.* Amsterdam: Global Reporting Initiative.

Hart, M. (1998-2010). What is an indicator of sustainability? Retrieved from:
    http://www.sustainablemeasures.com/node/89

Moffat, A. (2010). *The 21ˢᵗ century corporation: the ceres roadmap for sustainability.*
    Boston: Creative Commons.

SIGMA Project. (2003). *The SIGMA guidelines, putting sustainable development into
    practice – a guide for organizations.* London: AccountAbility, British
    Standards Institution and Forum for the Future.

United Nations Global Compact. The ten principles. Retrieved from:
    http://www.unglobalcompact.org/AboutTheGC/TheTenPrinciples/e
    nvironment.html

Chapter 8

Social Well-being

Hire the best. Pay them fairly. Communicate frequently. Provide challenges and rewards. Believe in them. Get out of their way and they'll knock your socks off.

—*Mary Ann Allison*

Introduction

In their excellent book, *Beyond Good Company* (Googins, Mirvis, & Rochlin, 2007, pp. 118-121), the authors describe IBM's wake-up call regarding social values and internal management systems. After generations spent on the cutting edge of development in the early 1990s—with the company slogan "THINK"—IBM suddenly approached collapse. In response, IBM made a major shift from hardware development to software and consulting, and they also took on their own internal management systems.

Beginning in the late 1980s and into the 1990s, IBM's internal management systems had lost their direction. Promises were regularly broken regarding career plans, new programs, and funding for projects. Those on the inside referred to IBM as "I've Been Misled" (p. 118). Morale had reached a low point.

Then, under new leadership that included Lou Gerstner in 1993 followed by Sam Palmisano in 2002, the company made a turnaround. They concentrated on working from within to develop values that resonated with their employees, using online "jam sessions" to engage employees from all over the world through their internal communication systems. Using trained moderators and sophisticated text analysis tools, they were able to find key themes among the employees' exchanges. One site was dedicated to positive values. It promoted thinking about what it was that made employees proud to be part of IBM and describing how they felt when the company was at its best.

As a result, IBM formulated their three core values (p. 119):

- Dedication to every client's success;
- Innovation that matters, for the company and the world; and
- Trust and personal responsibility in all relationships.

Former CEO Sam Palmisano noted the importance of developing these values from within rather than as an edict from above. By focusing on these values, IBM began to link its technologies to outside stakeholders including think tanks, NGOs, government agencies, and other companies.

Today, IBM is connecting its own product groups to research centers around the world to promote cross-fertilization of ideas beyond its own boundaries. This more open-minded attitude has not only motivated its own employees, it has also brought in fresh ideas from other companies and other cultures.

Social "Responsibility"

As with environmental stewardship, social well-being is affected by environmental attention and economic resources. It is therefore difficult to focus on social responsibility by itself. However, there are some widely accepted principles and guidelines that concentrate on social responsibility. We will look at some of those here.

The Earth Charter (mentioned in the previous chapter regarding environmental principles) characterizes social responsibility in terms of a number of principles. The preamble to the Earth Charter states that these principles are meant to apply to all individuals and organizations, including businesses (Earth Charter Initiative, 2000) (emphasis added):

- *Eradicate poverty* as an ethical, social, and environmental imperative
- Ensure that economic activities and institutions at all levels *promote human development in an equitable and sustainable manner*

- Affirm *gender equality and equity* as prerequisites to sustainable development and ensure universal access to education, health care, and economic opportunity
- Uphold the right of all, without discrimination, to a natural and social environment supportive of human dignity, bodily health, and spiritual well-being, with *special attention to the rights of indigenous peoples and minorities*
- *Strengthen democratic institutions* at all levels and provide transparency and accountability in governance, inclusive participation in decision making, and access to justice
- *Integrate into formal education and life-long learning* the knowledge, values, and skills needed for a sustainable way of life
- *Treat all living beings with respect* and consideration
- Promote a *culture of tolerance, nonviolence, and peace*

Environmental principles from the United Nations Global Compact were mentioned in the previous chapter. Their principles concerning the areas of human rights and labor are as follows (United Nations Global Compact):

Human Rights Principles:
1. Businesses should support and respect the protection of internationally proclaimed human rights; and
2. Make sure they are not complicit in human rights abuses.

Labor Principles:
3. Businesses should uphold the freedom of association and the effective recognition of the right to collective bargaining;
4. The elimination of all forms of forced and compulsory labor;
5. The effective abolition of child labor; and
6. Eliminate discrimination in respect of employment and occupation.

Anti-Corruption (added in 2004):
10. Businesses should work against corruption in all its forms, including extortion and bribery.

Following these principles and going beyond the expectations thereof can mean better long-term success for a company. As noted by the authors of *Beyond Good Company*, a study by Joseph Bragdon found that among sixty companies with top credit ratings and growth rates, the top performers take better care of their "living assets," such as their employees, communities, customers, and the environment (Googins, Mirvis & Rochlin, 2007, p. 119).

As we saw in the IBM example, such companies include their employees in this realm of social responsibility. How can a business expand these principles beyond just philanthropy to others outside of the company? How can they expand their social welfare principles to include the neighborhoods and communities where their facilities are located or even where their products are distributed? How do their actions affect their customer and supplier relationships? We'll wrestle with some of those questions here.

More Guidance from SIGMA

Human capital, as described in the SIGMA guidelines (2003, p. 17) from a business perspective, includes what is needed for people to be productive in the work force and to earn enough to achieve a better quality of life. It also includes qualities such as empathy, dignity, joy, spirituality, and passion. Organizations depend on human capital to function well and to therefore produce products and services efficiently. A healthy and motivated work force with the proper skills will certainly benefit any business. Intellectual capital and knowledge management are increasingly being recognized as key assets, even if it can be a challenge to put a hard value on these assets.

Any damage to human capital from the abuse of labor rights or health and safety issues can have not only direct impacts on business productivity but such issues can also can affect a company's reputation. In addition, poverty, crime, or other negative social circumstances can seriously impact the ability of a business to operate properly and to attract a quality work force. Paying attention to these important issues and investing in the work force as well as the local community can create real value for a company.

Social capital is described in the SIGMA guidelines (2003, p. 18) as value added to a business through human cooperation, relationships, and partnerships. This includes all sorts of human interaction, including interaction among families, communities, schools, and voluntary organizations as well as the more commonly considered networks and communication channels of businesses, trade associations, and communities. Social capital can also include cultural and social norms in addition to trust and social values. All of these interconnections represent a very important part of the success of any organization. Can you imagine what happens when trust and communication fail? Such a scenario can bring any organization to its knees, just as we saw in the IBM example above.

Within an organization, social capital can take the form of shared core values and norms as well as the communication of those values to help people work together in a cohesive and efficient manner. Looking out toward the community, a company can use these social structures to create a "license to operate" in a given area through community consent and support for the operations of the organization.

Finally, the wider sociopolitical structures of a community and society are also important. If a country is at war or if political anarchy is under way, it will be very difficult for any business or organization to function.

Accountability

As emphasized in the SIGMA guidelines, all social responsibility interests depend on the *accountability* of an organization. Once again, SIGMA helps us to sort out what this really means. Accountability consists of three elements (2003, p.4):

1. *Transparency:* The duty of an organization to be accountable to its stakeholders
2. *Responsiveness:* The need to respond to stakeholders
3. *Compliance:* The duty to comply with standards to which an organization is voluntarily committed and rules and regulations with which it must comply for statutory reasons

It might even be better to list these in reverse order. At a minimum, an organization should comply with any rules and regulations applicable to its activities. Next, it should respond to the needs and desires of its stakeholders. And finally, it should be transparent about communicating with its various constituencies. Engaging with these constituencies enables an organization to truly determine what is important and thereby improve its performance. This allows a company to stay ahead of its competitors in the field—by understanding what its customers want and by maintaining a happy and productive work force to produce those products.

The accountability principle therefore includes more than just being responsible; it includes being *responsive*, which means being innovative, nimble, insightful, and understanding. Accountability enables better evaluation and management of risks and opportunities, including liability and lawsuits from customers or employees, or market-related issues such as reputation and branding. Finally, accountability enhances financial capital by supporting overall improvements in performance and creating long-term value for both investors and owners.

How to Measure? — Social Indicators

As is the case with environmental indicators, there are a number of ways to measure progress from the social welfare perspective. GRI includes a number of suggested indicators for companies, including items such as employee turnover, health benefits, injuries and lost workdays, training and education programs, and disciplinary practices. Here are a few sample social indicators from the GRI guidelines (GRI, 2000-2011):

Labor Practices and Decent Work Performance Indicators (pp. 31-32)

LA1	Total work force by employment type, employment contract, and region, broken down by gender
LA15	Return to work and retention rates after parental leave, by gender
LA9	Health and safety topics covered in formal agreements with trade unions
LA10	Average hours of training per year per employee, by gender and by employee category
LA14	Ratio of basic salary and remuneration of women to men by employee category, by significant locations of operation

Human Rights Performance Indicators (p. 35)

HR4	Total number of incidents of discrimination and corrective actions taken

HR6   Operations and significant suppliers identified as having significant risk for incidents of child labor and measures taken to contribute to the effective abolition of child labor

Society Performance Indicators (p. 38)

SO9   Operations with significant potential or actual negative impacts on local communities

SO3   Percentage of employees trained in organization's anti-corruption policies and procedures

SO6   Total value of financial and in-kind contributions to political parties, politicians, and related institutions by country

Product Responsibility Performance Indicators (p. 39)

PR1   Life-cycle stages in which health and safety impacts of products and services are assessed for improvement and percentage of significant products and services categories subject to such procedures

PR5   Practices related to customer satisfaction, including results of surveys measuring customer satisfaction

A complete listing can be found on the GRI website, which is referenced in the supplementary reading section at the end of this chapter. The GRI guidelines have become a widely accepted reporting format for companies all over the world. Their lists are updated every couple of years through a public comment process involving a wide variety of contributors.

In addition to the GRI guidelines, we can consider the broader sustainability indicators developed by Maureen Hart, who was also mentioned in the last chapter. Table 8.1 below shows her perspective on indicators from the social perspective.

Table 8.1: Comparison of Traditional and Sustainability Social Indicators

(http://www.sustainablemeasures.com/node/90)

Social Indicators		
Traditional Indicators	**Sustainability Indicators**	**Emphasis of Sustainability Indicators**
SAT and other standardized test scores	Number of students trained for jobs that are available in the local economy Number of students who go to college and come back to the community	Matching job skills and training to needs of the local economy
Number of registered voters	Number of voters who vote in elections Number of voters who attend town meetings	Participation in democratic process Ability to participate in the democratic process

It is helpful to look at these hybrid indicators to spur thoughts among your colleagues. What are the particular aspects of your company that have significant impacts on society? How can you best measure those impacts and how can you tell if you are making progress? What are the most important or material interests of your stakeholders? Are there different types of indicators that you can compile yourself to measure your impacts and your progress? The lists of published indicators should help to get you started, but there may be internal indicators that you could develop to further your analysis.

Management Standards

There are a number of management standards that have been developed to help companies embed social sustainability into their organizations. With the establishment in 2010 of ISO 26000, guidance on social responsibility, organizations now have an internationally vetted tool with which to improve their approach to sustainability from a social perspective. This standard is a guidance document; it offers a framework that a company may use to develop a customized plan. It is not a standard to be certified against by a third party. Nevertheless, it can provide meaningful benefits to any company that pursues its guidelines.

The goal of the ISO 26000 document is to help companies understand and respect societal and cultural differences, as well as legal, economic, and environmental conditions where they operate and where their products or services are located. It provides guidance about engaging with stakeholders and developing more credible communication with and reports for those stakeholders, as well as broadening a basic awareness of social responsibility. The ISO 26000 framework is meant to complement existing systems within a company as well as legal standards and international treaties. Finally, it emphasizes performance results and continuous improvement, helping companies to improve their quality of products and services as well as their impact on society and the planet (ISO, 2010a).

The ISO guidance document emphasizes the importance of stakeholder identification and engagement coupled with the recognition of social responsibility from the organization's perspective and sphere of influence. It lists seven basic principles of social responsibility (ISO, 2010b, p. ix):

- Accountability
- Transparency
- Ethical behavior
- Respect for stakeholder interests
- Respect for the rule of law
- Respect for international norms of behavior
- Respect for human rights

The organization is instructed to apply these principles to each of the areas affecting its own operations, including human rights, labor practices, the environment, fair operating practices, consumer issues, and community involvement and development. By analyzing its own operations and processes in each of these areas, a company can develop its own plan to improve its operations with respect to the social well-being of those that it impacts. By using the framework of this standard, the company can make social responsibility integral to its culture and vision, building competencies throughout the organization to support the principles and issues that are most significant to its operations (ISO, 2010, p. ix).

As stated in the standard, employees are often the most important group of stakeholders to be considered with respect to human rights. For multinational companies with extended supply chains, this consideration can extend to countries where human rights protections and enforcement are lax. Companies are encouraged to take a leadership role and to use their sphere of influence with suppliers, and even competitors, to facilitate education and enforcement of human rights policies (ISO, 2010, p. 24).

Once again, the ISO 26000 guidance is not prescriptive. It does not require a certain percentage of female employees or a certain number of weeks of paid vacation. It does require companies to comply with applicable local and international laws and regulations, but beyond that, it is up to the company itself to set its own measureable goals and to work within its own organization to build a framework for management and continuous improvement.

Combining the ISO 26000 standard with other management systems such as ISO 14001 (environmental management) and OHSAS 18001 (occupational health and safety) can result in a robust management system that ensures the organization is fulfilling its goals not only for social well-being of its stakeholders but also environmental stewardship.

Concluding Thoughts

The emphasis on using standards and systems may seem like an extra step for an organization, but any business has its own management systems and procedures already in place. Referencing these internationally accepted standards, weaving them into the organization's framework and existing systems, will enable the company to tighten communication between various groups. Involving employees at all levels of the company is crucial. The CEO and management team drive improvements, but often some of the most creative ideas for improvements and problem solving can come from those working on the factory floor or in the office pool. The management systems mentioned encourage this type of cross-pollination and the company will be stronger and more resilient as a result.

Supplementary Reading Suggestions

GRI's guidelines represent the result of multi-stakeholder participation from individuals and organizations around the world. The GRI guidelines and other sustainability reporting resources can be found at their website:

https://www.globalreporting.org/Pages/default.aspx

ISO publishes a number of standards applicable to various areas of business. Their numbering system ensures compatibility across various languages and cultures. Developed by technical committees that span the globe and distributed for public comment before finalization, ISO standards are widely used by businesses worldwide. ISO 26000 (guidance on social responsibility) and other standards can be purchased and downloaded from the ISO website:

http://www.iso.org/iso/home.html.

The SIGMA Guidelines and other SIGMA Project publications are highly recommended as background reading and as a source for useful guidelines and tools. They are available for free download at:

http://www.projectsigma.co.uk/default.asp.

References

Earth Charter Initiative. (2000). The earth charter. Retrieved from
http://www.earthcharterinaction.org/content/pages/Read-the-Charter.html
Global Reporting Initiative (GRI). (2000-2011). *RG, sustainability reporting guidelines, version 3.1.* Amsterdam: Global Reporting Initiative.
Googins, B., Mirvis, P, & Rochlin, S. (2007). *Beyond good company; next generation corporate citizenship.* New York: Palgrave MacMillan.
International Organization for Standardization (ISO). (2010a). ISO social responsibility: about the standard. Retrieved from: http://www.iso.org
International Organization for Standardization (ISO). (2010b). *ISO 26000: guidance on social responsibility.* Available from: http://www.iso.org
SIGMA Project. (2003). *The SIGMA guidelines, putting sustainability into practice – a guide for organizations.* London: AccountAbility, British Standards Institution and Forum for the Future.
United Nations Global Compact. The ten principles. Retrieved from:
http://www.unglobalcompact.org/AboutTheGC/TheTenPrinciples/environment.html

Chapter 9

Economic Prosperity

I never wanted to be a businessman. I just wanted to change the world.
— *Richard Branson*

Introduction

Let's loop back to Ray Anderson again just for a moment. This topic makes me think of another story that Ray shares in his book, *Confessions of a Radical Industrialist* (2007, pp. 152-155). He describes a time in the late 1990s after the sustainability initiatives were well in place. A new management team at Interface had allowed Ray to step back from day-to-day company management in order to focus on his larger vision of sustainability. Interface had roughly doubled in size from 1993 to 1998 and spirits were high.

Then, an unexpected series of events occurred that almost crushed the company. First, one of their competitors, Shaw Industries, established its own exclusive network of carpet installers. Shortly thereafter, DuPont, one of Interface's major suppliers of yarn and fibers, also formed its own installer network. The assumption was that these suppliers would only be loyal to the companies with whom they were connected. What to do?

The Interface management team decided that the best response was to form its own installation system—to fight fire with fire. After all, they were riding high on their accomplishments and who wouldn't want to join the Interface team? Unfortunately, this choice did not turn out well. They ultimately committed $150 million to the purchase of a number of installation companies, but attempting to assimilate them into the Interface company system brought a plethora of problems—from record keeping to customer relations, many of which were personal to those installers. It was a disaster. Some of the installers realized a 50 percent drop in revenue. Interface saw a sharp decrease as well.

Interface held tough while many sales associates and installers said so long. By the time the dust settled, half of Interface's new management team had left as well. Ray Anderson returned home and took charge once again, this time with a wiser and more open-minded management team—more "humble," as he describes it (p. 154).

Ray Anderson tells this story as a lesson in fairness and respect. Focusing on just the economic results, as his experience reveals, can backfire. As Anderson explains, Interface forgot about respecting the needs of their people and the need to treat them fairly. Instead of patiently involving a variety of stakeholders (such as their independent installers) in the decision regarding how best to handle the DuPont and Shaw Industry competition, they boldly moved forward creating their own, exclusive installation force, a move that proved to be a brash and massive failure.

Fortunately for Interface, all the work they had already done to address energy efficiency, waste control, and pollution reduction helped them through their rocky time. They eventually recovered their position in the market, although their exclusive installation system did not survive. What happened initially sparked what seemed like a natural economic response, but in retrospect, it went exactly against the principles that Interface had formulated. Lessons learned, as we all say. Interface emerged chagrined but wiser and more committed than ever before.

Staying in Business

Part (a *big* part) of what every business owner wants is to stay in business—to be sustainable from an economic perspective. If a tried and true formula existed for doing so, every company would sign up. Unfortunately, that is not the case. Companies rise and fall. Economies boom and go bust. Both internal and external factors are at play with many different variables interacting.

Economists have developed various theories concerning how to keep people employed and economies moving forward, but such theories present an evolving and eternal debate. Raise taxes and stimulate through government spending or lower taxes and encourage private investment? Don't worry. We're not entering that debate here.

For businesses, the ultimate goal is to be profitable. Businesses seek to perform a service and pay a fair wage, to be sure, and to manage resources responsibly (at least from an economic standpoint), but ultimately to be profitable in the end. They pay dividends to their shareholders and hope that their share price remains stable and grows in value in order to provide continuing capital for future growth and profits.

But the economics of a business extend beyond its own walls. Having a stable supply of talented employees means having good schools and a healthy community such that those employees will want to live nearby. It also means providing a safe and healthy place where those employees and their families can live, including adequate transportation and housing, and maybe even a few good places to eat. These are both short-term and long-term benefits for a business. Without them, a business cannot sustain itself.

These benefits are not always included, however, on a business financial statement. Most businesses value their net worth from the perspective of profit, dividends, assets, return on investment, market capitalization, and book value. These all measure *past performance* (Doane & MacGillivray, 2001).

Certainly, trends in past performance can give investors an idea of future viability. But what about other external factors? How is the company communicating with its customers? Do they have a strategic plan to introduce new products that consumers will want? Are they listening to and engaging with important stakeholders? Are they outsourcing some of their products in factories overseas where employees are treated unfairly? Are they resourcing materials from countries where people are mistreated? Are these numbers telling the full story?

What happens when a competitor throws you a curve ball like what happened to Interface in 1998? How can you ensure that your management team has the capability to react? These are the types of questions that companies are beginning to ask internally. Those on the cutting edge are beginning to understand how to strengthen their internal management systems in order to plan ahead and prepare for the unexpected.

Sustainable Economic Indicators

GRI has helped to bridge the gap between traditional financial measurements and those that might help predict future performance. These indicators have already been mentioned in the two previous chapters. GRI addresses three areas of reporting—environmental, social, and economic. By including all three indicators and modeling them after generally accepted accounting principles, GRI is attempting to put environmental and social reporting on a level playing field with financial information and reporting.

Standardizing company reporting helps to bring some of the quantitative measures under the same reporting procedures as the qualitative measures. About half of GRI's questions are quantitative—for example, revenues, operating costs, salaries, donations, and other community investments. But other questions are qualitative, such as hiring procedures for hiring from the local community and policies for purchasing from local suppliers (Savitz, 2006, p. 212).

The reporting indicators listed in the economic section of GRI's guidelines also emphasize the organization's impact on the greater economic system in which it operates. GRI asks for additional contextual information regarding risks and opportunities, key successes or shortcomings, and any key strategies for improving performance or implementing policies (GRI, 2000-2011, pp. 25-26).

Getting this information into the financial statements is another challenge. However, there is a movement toward a "one report" system according to which many companies are now combining their sustainability reports with their annual reports. Those looking for straight financial information will therefore see sustainability information as well, whether they like it or not.

The *triple bottom line* may or may not be a current reality, and debate abounds as to whether this is just a slogan or a dream. However, given the GRI guidelines, businesses now have a clear roadmap regarding how to report on all three aspects of sustainability including more qualitative aspects of economic indicators.

Following are those aspects considered reportable under the GRI 3.1 guidelines. You can see that they include both records of past performance, such as revenues and expenses, as well as indicators of future performance, such as implications from climate change, local hiring procedures, and investments in local infrastructure (GRI, 2000-2011, p. 26):

ASPECT: ECONOMIC PERFORMANCE

EC1   Direct economic value generated and distributed, including revenues, operating costs, employee compensation, donations and other community investments, retained earnings, and payments to capital providers and governments

EC2   Financial implications and other risks and opportunities for the organization's activities due to climate change

EC3   Coverage of the organization's defined benefit plan obligations

EC4   Significant financial assistance received from government

ASPECT: MARKET PRESENCE

EC5   Range of ratios of standard entry-level wage by gender compared to local minimum wage at significant locations of operation

EC6   Policy, practices, and proportion of spending on locally based suppliers at significant locations of operation

EC7   Procedures for local hiring and proportion of senior management hired from the local community at locations of significant operation

ASPECT: INDIRECT ECONOMIC IMPACTS

EC8   Development and impact of infrastructure investments and services provided primarily for public benefit through commercial, in-kind, or pro bono engagement

EC9   Understanding and describing significant indirect economic impacts, including the extent of impacts

Once again, it's also a thought-provoking exercise to consider Maureen Hart's perspective on indicators shown in table 9.1 below. She continues to emphasize connections between the indicators themselves and the local community, though you can also see some similarities with the GRI indicators listed above.

Table 9.1: Economic Indicators and Sustainability
(http://www.sustainablemeasures.com/node/90)

Economic Indicators		
Traditional Indicators	**Sustainability Indicators**	**Emphasis of Sustainability Indicators**
Median income Per capita income relative to the US average	Number of hours of paid employment at the average wage required to support basic needs	What wage can buy Defines basic needs in terms of sustainable consumption
Unemployment rate Number of companies Number of jobs	Diversity and vitality of local job base Number and variability in size of companies Number and variability of industry types Variability of skill levels required for jobs	Resilience of the job market Ability of the job market to be flexible in times of economic change
Size of the economy as measured by Gross National Product and GDP	Wages paid in the local economy that are spent in the local economy Dollars spent in the local economy that pay for local labor and local natural resources Percent of local economy based on renewable local resources	Local financial resilience

Finally, some important indicators come from performance frameworks, which emphasize quality performance for a business. There are many such frameworks around the world and they share similar goals, including leadership, strategic planning, attention to employees and customers, focus on process and operations, as well as analysis and results.

As mentioned previously, one of the leading programs in the United States is the Baldrige Performance for Excellence Program. Their *Criteria for Performance Excellence*, updated and published every two years or so, provides an excellent framework for any business or organization. As with many other standards or performance frameworks, it is not prescriptive, but it offers an outline and a basis against which an organization can score itself and spur future improvement.

The Baldrige Criteria provide more questions than answers. They can therefore incite discussion and help companies to get out of the habit of looking at financial data (past performance) alone. Combining various indicators can better support planning and long-term decisions (future performance). In the knowledge management section the Baldrige Criteria ask questions such as the following (2011-2012, p. 16):

> Performance Measures
> * How do you select, collect, align, and integrate data and information for tracking daily operations and overall organizational performance, including progress relative to strategic objectives and action plans?
> * What are your key organizational performance measures, including key short-term and longer-term financial measures?
> * How frequently do you track these measures?
> * How do you use these data and information to support organizational decision making and innovation?

The Baldrige Criteria encourage the use of multiple forms of data analysis, including not only financial and market data, but also customer data, information from competitors (including benchmarking), and operational information. All of this should become part of strategic planning for the organization (2011-2012, p. 17).

Valuing Reputation

Putting a value on reputation or "brand" is becoming more commonplace—finally. When I majored in economics as an undergrad in the late 1970s, I was taught that there was no way to value "company goodwill," as it was called back then. Today, it is established that brands have value, but exactly how to estimate that value remains a bit elusive.

Interbrand, a leading international consulting firm on branding, has evaluated over twenty-five hundred brands using a methodology that combines three factors: predicted future earnings, the connection of the brand to those earnings, and the risk profile of the brand and its expected earnings. This approach appears to have sound footing, but critics still claim that it is hard to prove. Nonetheless, this methodology represents a beginning in an important area of company valuation (Doane & MacGillivray, 2001, p. 36).

Economic Responsibility and the Process View

When considering the economic processes of a business, it helps to focus on two of the five capitals: manufactured capital and financial capital. The SIGMA guidelines can once again provide some direction.

Manufactured capital, as described in the SIGMA guidelines (2003, p. 19), refers to the materials and the infrastructure used in the production of goods that don't actually become a part of those goods. So things like tools, machines, buildings, and technology—all forms of infrastructure owned or leased by the business—can be referred to as manufactured capital.

The employment of manufactured capital can contribute to sustainability when it is used wisely and efficiently, and when it provides flexibility and innovative solutions to product manufacturing. By being creative with technology, the use of resources can be reduced or even eliminated, thereby enhancing the business's competitive advantage.

Financial capital, which is also described well in the SIGMA guidelines (2003, p. 21), includes the obvious: the actual monetary currency and financial assets such as stocks, bonds, and bank notes. But financial capital also includes the value that is created by the other four types of capital—environmental, social, human, and manufactured—that are under the control of the business.

As mentioned above, businesses are certainly measured by their monetary performance and success. But truly sustainable organizations understand that financial capital depends on the performance of the other forms of capital. These companies make an effort to assign financial value to contributions from the other four capital types as well. It is therefore important to understand the links between the capital types, including how each can be maintained from a "principal" standpoint. That is, using just the interest earned on the principal, or earnings from the capital invested rather than dipping into the principal itself. This preserves the company's capital for future operations. The GRI guidelines and indicators can help with this assessment.

Risk Management and Sarbanes-Oxley

Circling back to the basics, companies need to manage various minimum requirements in order to reduce the risk of government sanction or lawsuits. The Sarbanes-Oxley Act of 2002, passed in the US Congress largely in response to the Enron and WorldCom scandals, represents an important financial reporting requirement for large corporations. It requires more transparency and greater financial control by management with the aim to restore shareholder, investor, and public trust in publicly traded companies.

Developing appropriate governance systems and internal control mechanisms constitute an important part of complying with Sarbanes-Oxley. Such systems also help to predict and manage other business operation risks. And as you might have guessed, there are management systems available to help businesses develop these internal controls and to better control risk.

The field of enterprise risk management relies on two commonly used frameworks: the Turnbull framework, developed in 1999 in the United Kingdom, and the COSO framework, developed in 2004 in the United States by the Committee of Sponsoring Organizations of the Treadway Commission (COSO). Each of these frameworks provide for risk identification and assessment, response, monitoring and control, and implementation through board and management system integration (Roberts, 2005).

ISO has also published a risk management standard, ISO 31000 (2009). This standard outlines a framework with which an organization can understand its own risks given the context of its operations and thereafter embed its risk management processes into the culture of the organization, making those processes an integral part of management operations. The ISO standard requires communication with stakeholders to ensure that risks are identified properly, as well as monitoring and review to ensure that the organization learns from the process and improves its procedures (ISO, 2009, p. 13).

Although managing risk is important for any company, there are those who argue that companies should go beyond risk management and also plan forward strategies built on brand and customer loyalty. By fully analyzing their market share, customer service levels, and product development (through robust stakeholder engagement), companies can move beyond managing crises to avoiding crises altogether.

Using a balanced scorecard (see Chapter 4), companies can measure business objectives and results across the company including more than just financial information. This methodology combines traditional financial results with more predictive information, including customer impact, employee satisfaction, and innovation. Although the traditional balanced scorecard was not designed to include environmental and social concerns, it can be modified to include these objectives (Doane & MacGillivray, 2001, p. 34).

Concluding Thoughts

It is interesting to think about economic sustainability. Although it is the most emphasized part of business success from a mainstream point of view, it may ultimately be the most elusive of the three aspects of sustainability. Can a business survive economically without respecting the environmental and social aspects of its operations? Can the traditional financial measurements truly predict the long-term health of a business or are other leading indicators needed, such as investments in environmental and social resources? How can an organization best invest in those resources and how should the organization measure those investments? These are the questions that modern economists and sustainability professionals are embracing together. It is a fascinating exercise and the good news is that there are a lot of smart people contributing to the debate.

More and more, mature companies are realizing that managing the various pieces of information about a company in separate "silos" is neither the most efficient nor the most beneficial approach. Even economic management can be separated into various components of finance, investor relations, communications, human resources, upper-level management, and the board. Looking beyond short-term, quarterly planning toward long-range planning for stability is becoming a more viable, more accepted approach (Doane & MacGillivray, 2001, p. 48).

Working in tandem with the environmental and socially conscious departments in the organization and engaging with important stakeholders, companies can truly get beyond risk management and move toward innovation and collaboration. Mainstreaming economic management systems can be improved by including the perspectives of others throughout the organization.

Supplementary Reading Suggestions

There is an excellent commentary on economic reporting and its evolution in sustainability, which includes charts and tables comparing various reporting techniques as well as a very interesting graph showing the trends of business "churns" (going out of business or merging) and the number of overall companies listed on the London Stock exchange over the past thirty years (on page 21 of the referenced document). See:

> Doane, D. & MacGillivray, A. (2001). Economic sustainability: the business of staying in business. The SIGMA Project. Retrieved from:
> http://projectsigma.co.uk/RnDStreams/RD_economic_sustain. pdf

For more information on enterprise risk management and how it can be integrated into a business system, refer to this excellent white paper:

> Roberts, H. (2004). *Enterprise Risk Management: A long-term solution for compliance, governance, and sustained growth in shareholder value.* Available for free download at:
> http://www.coso.org/documents/COSO_ERM_ExecutiveSum mary.pdf

Besides the GRI framework referenced in the last two chapters (also recommended for reading here), the Baldrige Criteria provide many good business guidelines. Although its emphasis is quality performance, it includes many areas that would improve a business seeking to mainstream sustainability into its operations. Whether or not a business seeks recognition under this program, its guidelines remain sound.

> Baldrige National Quality Program. (2011-2012). *Criteria for performance excellence.* Gaithersburg, MD: National Institute of Standards and Technology. Available for free download at:
> http://www.nist.gov/baldrige/publications/upload/2011_2012 _Business_Nonprofit_Criteria.pdf

References

Anderson, R.C. (2009). *Confessions of a radical industrialist: profits, people, purpose – doing business by respecting the earth.* New York: St. Martin's Press.

Baldrige National Quality Program. (2011-2012). *Criteria for performance excellence.* Gaithersburg, MD: National Institute of Standards and Technology.

Doane, D. & MacGillivray, A. (2001). Economic sustainability the business of staying in business. The SIGMA Project. Retrieved from:
http://projectsigma.co.uk/RnDStreams/RD_economic_sustain.pdf

Global Reporting Initiative (GRI). (2000-2011). *RG, sustainability reporting guidelines, version 3.1.* Amsterdam: Global Reporting Initiative.

International Organization for Standardization (ISO). (2009). *ISO 31000: risk management – principles and guidelines.* Geneva: International Organization for Standardization.

Roberts, H. (2005). *Enterprise risk management: a long-term solution for compliance, governance, and sustained growth in shareholder value.*

Savitz, A.W. (2006). *The triple bottom line: how today's best-run companies are achieving economic, social, and environmental success – and how you can too.* San Francisco: Josey-Bass.

SIGMA Project. *The SIGMA guidelines – toolkit.* London: AcountAbility, BSI, Forum for the Future. Retrieved from www.projectsigma.com.

Chapter 10

Corporate Sustainability Strategy

The essence of environmental strategy is to make it an issue for your competitor, not for your own company...because you've already made sustainability an integral part of your business.
— Amory Lovins, Rocky Mountain Institute

Introduction

Sustainability strategy is becoming more and more important in today's world of constrained resources, population growth pressures, and financial unpredictability amid a climate that is becoming more dangerous to the health of the earth's ecosystems. Companies on the leading edge of sustainability strategy will be more likely to succeed in this uncertain world going forward.

Some are taking a bold stance on emission reductions, such as Frito-Lay with its zero-emissions potato chip plant in Arizona. Owned by PepsiCo, the company underwent a strategy planning process to pick the right manufacturing plant where they could take a significant stand on energy, water, and waste management. The result has not only proven that it can be done (and done so profitably), but it has also addressed the complicated systems and improved processes for plants around the world.

The Frito-Lay Arizona plant has not yet accomplished its goal of net zero emissions, but it has installed various solar power systems that now generate half of its electricity needs (including shading the parking lot for employee cars); recycled 75 percent of its water use (critical in the Arizona desert); reduced natural gas use by 80 percent (by installing a boiler that burns factory and regional bio waste); and reduced landfill waste to zero (including employee recycling incentives throughout the plant). The facility has a Leadership in Energy and Environmental Design (LEED) Gold rating, which is a respectable accomplishment, but is even more impressive given that the building is twenty-eight years old.

Al Halverson, PepsiCo's senior sustainability director, has explained that the company envisioned putting together a plant that combined all of the best sustainability operations they had developed around the world. They looked at their various facilities and picked the Arizona plant as a model where they could satisfy their vision for taking a manufacturing plant off the grid of electricity, water, and waste management (Fusaro, 2012).

Even though they make potato chips, which could spark a separate conversation on social responsibility and snack foods, Frito-Lay demands our respect for their foresight. We need more companies like this, companies who push ahead of their competition and bring sustainability to a global scale in order to prevent the kinds of cliffs predicted by leading sociologists, climatologists, and even economists. Sociologists argue that empowering and educating women will naturally and pragmatically slow population growth. Environmentalists argue that dramatically increasing resource efficiency and renewal is needed to avoid significant damage to our natural resources (Lubber, 2010). And McKinsey & Company reported in 2009 that the potential exists to stabilize climate emissions to a two-degree rise in global temperatures at manageable costs estimated at 1 percent of global GDP (McKinsey & Co., 2009, p. 14).

How Strategy Works

Every successful company performs strategy planning. Some do it as an ongoing, rotating process while others conduct major strategy planning sessions every three years or so with minor adjustments in the off years. For a large company, strategy planning needs to be managed from the executive suite and then pushed out to the various operations of the company with specific planning efforts taking place at each level, coordinated from the top. The goal is to drive the company's strategy into the fabric of the company, making it a part of each of its various activities and operations.

For any business, planning is the first and most important step. As William Blackburn explains, "failure to plan is planning to fail" (Blackburn, 2007, p. 189). He notes that without strategic planning, managers will simply devote company resources to whatever project they feel is most appropriate according to their own priorities. This can result in a tremendous waste of time, energy, and money, with the possibility of some divisions even working at cross-purposes. Certainly priorities are important, but they should be aligned with an overall business plan inclusive of stakeholder input and involvement in plan execution.

Some argue that all of this planning takes up too much time. When will we have time to do our real jobs? But planning can save enormous amounts of time in the long run. And, as Blackburn notes, a multinational study found that an average of eighty-seven working days are lost from inefficiency each year per person, mainly due to poor management planning and faulty execution oversight (2007, p. 189-190).

Although planning does take time away from actual production, in the end it can increase efficiency and productivity, identify important risks and opportunities, bring in new and creative ideas, and ensure accountability for quality performance across the organization (Blackburn, 2007, p. 190).

And, as Michael Porter states, a big part of planning can be deciding what you *don't* want to do, what's not important to the advancement of your business, or identifying those actions that take away from your primary emphasis. Making the company activities fit together is part of what the strategy process should accomplish—it ensures that all of a company's activities mutually reinforce each other rather than contradict or dilute what people think about when they envision that company. Porter uses the example of when Continental Lite tried to imitate only portions of Southwest Airlines' offerings. Their endeavor ended in disaster (Porter, 1996).

Making these decisions takes discipline and leadership as well as clear communication across all levels of the organization. Even then you may not get it right. But investing the time and resources in a clearly organized strategy planning exercise offers a much better chance at success than going blindly down a road in the direction of what a few at the top think is best. Finding a path that top management and other leaders throughout the company can agree upon ensures a much better chance at real success. Employing the opinion of some key stakeholders in the process may pay off as well.

Incorporating sustainability into strategic planning can have the added benefit of increasing diversity and expertise at the board level. This may lead to better insight into sustainability planning at all levels of the organization, linking progress to employee compensation. This approach can also promote a more vigorous and productive dialogue with important stakeholders including NGOs, suppliers, investors, employees, and customers. Supporting transparency can lead to better tracking and reporting of company progress toward its sustainability goals. Finally, incorporating sustainability into strategic planning can promote systematic improvements across the company's value chain, leading to lower costs, more efficient use of resources, happier and more productive employees, and satisfied customers (Lubber, 2010).

Strategy Planning Process

First, set the goals and priorities. Most strategy gurus recommend that the process for strategy planning include both a top-down and a bottom-up process. This means that ideas should be collected from the field of operations at various levels, with goals and recommendations for their particular operations. Top management should then review these recommendations and collect them into a group of broad goals and priorities. This information should then be sent back down to the more granular, team levels to be more fully developed into team projects and priorities. Through coordination of these efforts, the management team can continue to oversee the overall strategy planning and make corrections along the way to ensure alignment of the planning process.

At this stage, it's best to focus on *what* the company wants to achieve, rather than getting caught up in the *how*. Blackburn (2007, p. 193) emphasizes that more creative ideas are important at this stage. Teams can get bogged down in the details if they begin to consider the steps needed to accomplish their goals too early in the planning process. It's not that the *how* isn't important, it's just that focusing on the details can prevent the necessary, whole-systems thinking that occurs when ideas are first generated. Later, groups of appropriate people can be assembled to figure out the best and most efficient *how*.

Next, prioritization. After the main goals and initiatives have been selected (usually to be accomplished within the next three to five years), it's time to prioritize. The organization's current capabilities and resources should be analyzed. What is possible and what resources will need to be devoted to these goals if implemented? Here is where some of the *how* can come into play. By developing an analysis of the strengths, weaknesses, opportunities, and threats involved with each goal (a simple "SWOT" analysis), goals that should move to the top will become more obvious (Blackburn, 2007, p.200).

Various tools are available to assist managers with reaching a consensus regarding goal prioritization. These tools include priority mapping according to value and resources, as shown in figure 10.1 below. In this case, the relative cost of resources and the relative value of the goal are mapped according to an informal rating system. High priorities are assigned a four and high cost items are rated at zero. Lower cost items are rated a four or somewhere in-between. This can be a somewhat subjective exercise, but when scores are received from various planners, they tend to average out. The end result should provide a useful graphic representation of those items that create the most value for the company using the least resources.

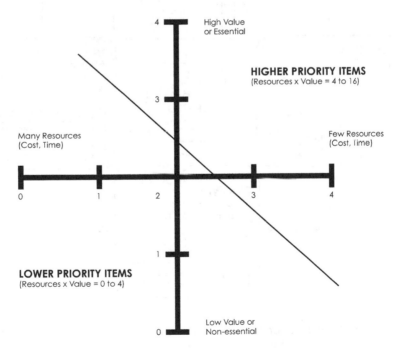

Figure 10.1: Priority Mapping: Value x Resources
(Adapted from Blackburn, 2007, p. 205)

Another useful tool used by many progressive companies is the balanced scorecard developed by Robert Kaplan and David Norton (also mentioned in Chapter 4). This tool helps to align an organization's corporate vision and mission with its strategy and business activities. The balanced scorecard can actually be used as a management system, driving vision and strategy into the operations of the company, and providing necessary feedback to management to enable analysis and to promote continuous improvement. Figure 10.2 below shows a basic outline of the balanced scorecard as envisioned by Kaplan and Norton (Balanced Scorecard Institute, 1998-2012).

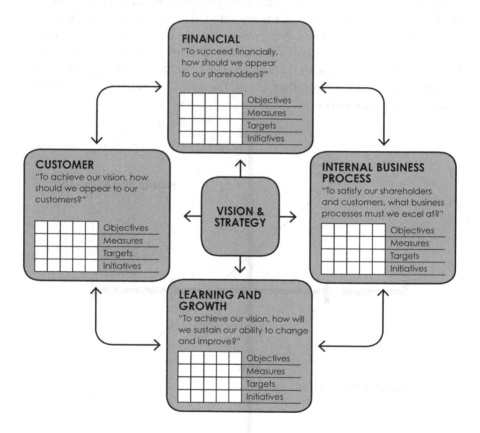

Figure 10.2: Balanced Scorecard as a Strategic Management System
(Balanced Scorecard Institute, 1998-2012)

When sustainability concerns are included in the vision and the mission of the company, sustainability may become a part of the whole strategy through the balanced scorecard framework.

Tactical planning and resources. After management determines the most important areas for strategy planning, it's time to work out the details. This includes making sure that necessary resources—both monetary resources and employees—are devoted to each objective. Without adequate resources and information, any plan is doomed to failure or may get left withering on the vine. If these assets are not available or are delayed, the plan should be modified or scaled back to ensure success. Otherwise, delays can result in wasted time and energy; delays may also discourage the progress of other important priorities. As William Blackburn states, "the rule should be, *if in doubt, cut it out*" (2007, p.213).

Listing the responsibilities associated with each action and attaching a timeline encourages accountability and ownership of the work to be performed. Even better results can be produced if those involved in the planning are those responsible for implementation. Then that person is moving his or her own ideas forward. Those involved in the implementation should also be allowed to participate in budgeting and scheduling (Blackburn, 2007, p. 214).

Risk analysis and aspects. Part of the planning process should also involve analysis of risks and potential impacts on the environment and society. This will come up more in the next chapter, where we will more closely examine the SMS as outlined by the various international standards, including ISO 14001 (environmental management) and ISO 26000 (guidance on social responsibility). Using these tools, an organization can identify the aspects of their production processes that have adverse or beneficial impacts on the environment or society. These frameworks help an organization to properly plan and implement the prioritized strategies developed during the strategy planning process.

Using Performance Frameworks

Performance frameworks like the Baldrige Criteria also emphasize the importance of strategy planning. The Baldrige Criteria use mostly questions organized into basic categories. Under strategy planning, the criteria include questions to help the company determine its key strengths, weaknesses, opportunities, and threats. By understanding these key positions, the organization can develop a plan to resolve some of its most important priorities and set goals for improvement.

As stressed by Blackburn, the Baldrige Criteria emphasize the efficiency gains from the strategy planning process. When a company better understands the resources needed to execute a plan, it will have those people and resources available when needed rather than having to scramble and reallocate those resources from other divisions or areas. Finally, the Baldrige Criteria help an organization to achieve effective implementation by providing leadership at the executive level, work system analysis at the process level, and appropriate guidance at the execution level of individual work units. This is extremely important. No strategic plan can be successful unless it accounts for execution and performance (Baldrige, 2011-2012, p. 27).

The Baldrige Criteria encourage the organization to interpret strategy planning broadly and to include the possibility of new products, new customer groups, core competencies, partnerships, or alliances, or to meet a new need in the market or community. In this sense, strategy planning could be directed toward a key supplier or major local supplier, or even a market innovator (Baldrige, 2011-2012, p. 10).

Like other frameworks, the Baldrige Criteria encourage the organization to make certain that it devotes adequate time, people, and resources to the strategy process. The criteria also note the linkages between strategy and leadership, stakeholder engagement, work force capability and education, and reporting and measurement processes (2011-2012, p. 12).

Concluding Thoughts

Many different strategy models and frameworks are available. This chapter mentions just a few. The value of these frameworks is that they offer a concrete method for organizing abstract ideas and provide tangible measurements and indicators. Such frameworks provide the management team with a structure to work within that can be customized to fit their goals and needs.

It is important to first measure where your organization stands and then to contrast that with where you want the organization to be. The strategy process helps to outline specific goals and objectives concerning how to get to that vision, both in the next few years and beyond.

As illustrated in the quote by Amory Lovins at the beginning of this chapter, strategy from an environmental (or sustainability) perspective can provide a competitive advantage. In today's world of ultra-communication, the reputation of companies who are seen as leaders in environmental and social responsibility is less at risk due to an increasingly aware consumer base. The strategic planning process itself may uncover risks and opportunities, helping a company to stay ahead in the areas of innovation and corporate responsibility. If you are truly pursuing the strategizing process, doing so becomes an issue for your competitors, not for you.

In the next chapter, we will delve more deeply into the *how* of implementing strategy. What specific measurement tools are available? What types of internal reporting are necessary? And how can you drive continuous improvement in the process? These are important questions and concepts for any company to master in its quest for excellence and balanced environmental, societal, and economic responsibility.

Supplementary Reading Suggestions

Harvard Business Review articles are carefully protected and must be purchased. However, their collection of "essential" strategy articles, *HBR Must-Reads on Strategy*, is available for purchase on their website for about twenty-five dollars. It includes the Michael Porter article cited in this chapter, as well as Robert Kaplan and David Norton's article, "Using the Balanced Scorecard as a Strategic Management System." This collection may be considered worth the investment. Here's the link:

> http://hbr.org/product/baynote/an/12601-PDF-ENG?referral=00506

Another popular model for strategy planning includes the 7-S Model (or the McKinsey 7-S), developed by Tom Peters and Robert Waterman while they were associated with McKinsey & Company. The 7-S stands for: structure, strategy, shared values, style, staff, skills, and systems. These are all interconnected and must be coordinated within the core of shared values for a successful strategy. A brief description and short video describing the 7-S Model can be found on the Mind Tolls website:

> http://www.mindtools.com/pages/article/newSTR_91.htm.

For more on the balanced scorecard, including a free white paper entitled, "Linking Sustainability to Corporate Strategy Using the Balanced Scorecard," consult the Balanced Scorecard Institute at:

> www.balancedscorecard.org.

The Baldrige Criteria are captured together in a rich document including many good guidelines for a business. The strategy section mentioned above contains many questions aimed at focusing on quality performance. It also contains sections on guidance and recommendations.

> Baldrige National Quality Program. (2011-2012). *Criteria for performance excellence.* Gaithersburg, MD: National Institute of Standards and Technology. Available for free download at: http://www.nist.gov/baldrige/publications/upload/2011_2012 _Business_Nonprofit_Criteria.pdf

References

Balanced Scorecard Institute. (1998-2012). Balanced scorecard basics. Retrieved from:
    http://www.balancedscorecard.org/BSCResources/AbouttheBalanced Scorecard/tabid/55/Default.aspx
Baldrige National Quality Program. (2011-2012). *Criteria for performance excellence.* Gaithersburg, MD: National Institute of Standards and Technology. Retrieved from: http://www.nist.gov/baldrige/
Blackburn, W. (2007). *The sustainability handbook.* Washington, DC: Environ- mental Law Institute.
Fusaro, D. (2012). PepsiCo Casa Grande plant reaches 'near net zero.' sustainable plant. Retrieved from:
    http://www.sustainableplant.com/2012/05/pepsico-casa-grande-plant-reaches-near-net-zero/?start=0
Lubber, M. (2010). 4 Keys to a successful sustainability strategy. GreenBiz.com. Retrieved from: http://www.greenbiz.com/blog/2010/03/15/4-keys-successful-sustainability-strategy
McKinsey & Company. (2009). Pathways to a low carbon economy. Retrieved from:
    http://webarchive.iiasa.ac.at/rains/meetings/Annex1/presentations/ mckinsey.pdf
Porter, M.E. (1996). What is strategy? *Harvard Business Review, 74*(6), 61-78.

Chapter 11

Sustainability Management System

Planning is an unnatural process; it is much more fun to do something. The nicest thing about not planning is that failure comes as a complete surprise, rather than being preceded by a period of worry and depression.

— Sir John Harvey-Jones

The time you want the map…is before you enter the woods.

— Brendon Burchard

Introduction

Our look at strategy in the last chapter introduced the idea of planning, which includes having a rigorous process for planning, implementation, and review of that strategy. An SMS is like a strategy on steroids. It infuses into an entire organization the notion of planning, implementing, keeping careful records, and then reviewing progress to ensure plan compliance while looking for areas of improvement.

We've already covered most of the major elements of an SMS in this book. Now it's time to put them all together to formulate an overall plan and implementation system. These elements can all be incorporated into a robust structure that can be customized for any business or its local operations. Making the SMS part of the business systems makes it operational at all levels of the company. It becomes part of what every employee thinks about every day as he or she makes decisions about the processes and services performed.

Rather than making a snap judgment with regards to a marketing decision, the marketing department will think about stakeholder engagement and how to better plan for the rollout of a product. Rather than seeking a quick fix on a pollution issue, the production team may bring in research and development representatives to see if processes can be improved overall to avoid such waste in the first place. Transportation issues can be considered from a more holistic perspective. Product design may include LCA. All of these ideas are supported through the use of a robust SMS thereby supporting teamwork, breaking down silos in the organization, and improving communication and coordination in accordance with the overall vision of the company.

Most SMS programs are based upon the basic plan-do-check-act framework presented in the international standard ISO 14001 (environmental management). This is the most commonly used standard and is often required by customers of their suppliers to ensure the presence of a basic management system and control of environmental hazards. The ISO 14001 framework can be combined with various other guidelines and standards to include social, economic, and quality improvement goals, and it can be further fleshed out in specific areas such as risk management (ISO 31000), energy management (ISO 51000), and occupational health and safety (OHSAS 18001). Start with the basic outline and then customize it to fit your particular organization.

In this chapter, we'll take a look at the four stages of the ISO 14001-based management system and how that system can be complemented by other frameworks and standards. It all starts with *planning* (here we go again) and is followed by *doing* (implementation), *checking* (recording and tracking progress), and finally, *acting* (an unfortunate label that really means comparing results and making plans for further improvement). Plan-do-check-act is common parlance in the sustainability world.

Plan-Do-Check-Act Summarized

The plan-do-check-act system rests first on the organization's firm commitment to sustainability goals. This must of course be accepted and adopted by top-level management, but it must also be confirmed at all levels of the organization. Using the system as it is outlined here enables a company to establish necessary objectives and processes to meet its policy commitments. The framework helps to make environmental and social impacts part of every decision that is made rather than becoming sidelined as separate initiatives.

PLAN (ISO, 2004, pp 4-5): After the goals and policies have been identified through the strategy process, the real planning begins. The strategy planning process is outlined in some detail in the previous chapter. For the SMS, planning should emphasize identifying specific aspects of the activities, services, or products of the company with environmental or social impacts. Which of these have the most significant impact? Second, what legal requirements are applicable to company activities? Third, what are the specific objectives and targets for improvement? And lastly, who will be responsible for overseeing the planning and implementation? This planning process involves people at all levels of the organization, in the kind of coordinated effort described in the last chapter.

Strategy planning and planning for the SMS can ideally be done together. Implementation and recording can then follow along with the rest of the SMS framework.

DO (ISO, 2004, pp. 5-7): This is the implementation stage of the SMS. Necessary resources need to be committed to the implementation process and appropriate roles and responsibilities must be assigned. Competency needs to be ensured among those responsible. Training programs must be arranged if there is a gap in leadership or capability. Adequate documentation and communication are necessary to ensure that both internal and external communication are sufficient. The control of documents and operational procedures must also be addressed. And finally, emergency plans should be prepared, to plan ahead of time for that day that no company wants to occur.

CHECK (ISO, 2004, pp. 7-8): The check phase includes monitoring and measuring progress, compliance with legal requirements and policy goals, and plans for dealing with non-conforming results (results that don't meet the goals and targets identified earlier). Procedures for control of records need to be established and an internal audit must be performed to confirm that all was done as planned.

ACT (ISO, 2004, p. 9): The last stage of plan-do-check-act involves review by top management of the entire process, including an evaluation of progress toward stated goals. Which goals were met and which were missed? Were there changes in the legal requirements along the way? Were there complaints or other input from stakeholders that should be incorporated into future plans? What are the recommendations for future improvement?

Figure 11.1 below provides a visual picture of the continuous cycle of plan-do-check-act.

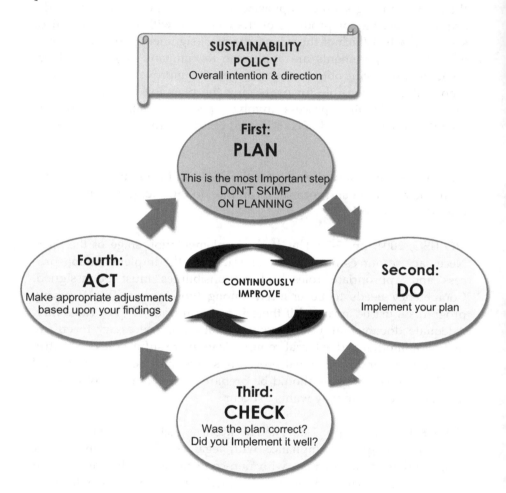

Figure 11.1: Plan-Do-Check-Act Cycle
(Adapted from ISO, 2004)

This may seem like a lot for an organization to undertake, but once again, the overall benefit of planning and implementation is to improve the company's operations. Having a well-articulated plan with specific, agreed-upon goals and then implementing that plan with adequate indicators and records will help the organization to improve its operations and increase productivity overall. Companies that embrace this practice simply perform better. As mentioned in Chapter 3 concerning the business case, the embracers of sustainability see it as a value center and make sustainability integral to every decision (MIT & BCG, 2009).

Plan-Do-Check-Act Unpacked

Sustainability Policy: As mentioned above, the overarching foundation of the SMS is establishing a sustainability policy. Ultimately, the sustainability policy for a company should be consistent with its overall

SUSTAINABILITY POLICY
Overall intention & direction

mission, vision, and core values as discussed in Chapter 5. But many companies choose to have a separate and more specific sustainability policy. This should include goals for both environmental stewardship and social well-being.

For example, Unilever, a long-time leader in sustainability, puts responsibility for social and environmental concerns at the top of its sustainability strategy as follows (Unilever, 2012):

> Unilever's future success depends upon being able to decouple our growth from our environmental footprint, while at the same time increasing our positive social impacts. These are the central objectives of the Unilever Sustainable Living Plan, which we launched in November 2010.

The Unilever policy is much more extensive and more detailed than quoted here. Their policy lists specific goals and reasons for the pursuit of those goals, including their own business case as well as examples of how sustainability has provided value and growth. They consider sustainability and profits to be mutually supportive.

According to the ISO requirement, a company's sustainability policy should be clearly communicated to all who are associated with the company, including employees, of course, but also contractors and others who represent the company at outlying facilities. The policy drives the SMS and it should be the basis upon which objectives and goals are set. The policy should be clear in scope and should reflect the unique nature of the company's products and services (ISO, 2004, p. 11).

Plan

Sustainability Footprint: The first step in the planning process is to determine the scope of the SMS. As mentioned in Chapter 4, it is important to understand the footprint of a company in terms of its processes and the context of its operations. This footprint is determined by defining the scope. It clarifies the boundaries of the SMS including all of the activities, products, and services performed by the organization. This must also be fair and reasonable. You can't leave out important areas just to relieve yourself of responsibility. If an important area is excluded, there must be an explanation provided for doing so.

First:
PLAN

This is the most Important step
DON'T SKIMP ON PLANNING:
- Sustainability Footprint
- Social and environmental aspects
- Legal and other requirements
- Objectives and targets

The scope of the SMS may include a specific operation or division of a company. Often companies will certify each facility to ISO 14001 as a start and then expand the facility to a full SMS under the company's direction. R.R. Donnelley, for example, has a number of printing facilities, which are owned by the parent company, that are ISO 14001 certified. This is a way to get started along the path to sustainability. Doing so brings each area of the company up toward the goal of higher standards.

For the company's sustainability footprint overall, the organization needs to consider the social and environmental impacts of its operations. An LCA may be used to understand the impacts in certain areas. The legal requirements must be considered as well as risks to regulation and reputation. These must be listed and then prioritized in order to find the most significant areas for action. Stakeholder engagement is a very important part of this process as the company needs to fully understand all of the risks involved. Input from stakeholders will help to prevent overlooking any important items.

Social and Environmental Aspects: After the scope and vision have been established, it is important to develop a comprehensive list of all of the environmental and social aspects that are under the company's control, either directly or indirectly. From an environmental perspective, this could include air emissions, water use or release, land use or waste, use of raw materials and other natural resources, energy use and emission of heat or radiation, and even the physical attributes of the building and its surroundings (ISO, 2004, pp. 11-12). Are there particular aspects of the company that are resource or energy intensive? Is there an alternate source of fuel available or can energy efficiencies be implemented? Has an LCA revealed that conflict minerals are contained in some of the company's products? Are rare earth materials used?

From a social perspective, aspects can include governance, human rights, labor practices, fair operating practices, consumer issues, community involvement and development, and social impacts from environmental aspects (ISO, 2010, p. 19). This is also a phase during which the ISO 31000 risk management standard can be incorporated in order to ensure that any important risks are not overlooked.

What are some of the social risks of the company? Are certain products outsourced to developing countries where labor laws are more lax or are less enforced than in the United States? Suppliers may sign a code of conduct, but is anyone checking to ensure that these policies are being followed? What would the ramifications be if the production of a key product in the supply chain were found to involve child labor?

Apple computer came under fire in the summer of 2012 for its handling of the manufacturing of products in China's Foxconn facilities. Foxconn manufactures goods for other companies as well, including Cisco, Huawei, Nintendo, Sony, and Nokia, but the controversy stuck to Apple as its major brand (Kan, M. 2012). How could Apple have prevented this scandal?

Corruption is another issue with which global companies wrestle. Walmart was in the news in the summer of 2012 for allegedly bribing public officials in Mexico in order to facilitate the construction of Walmart stores (see, for example, Martin, 2012). This was clearly against corporate policy, but what follow-up or auditing was performed to ensure that existing policies were being followed? Even though Walmart claimed to have already discovered the corruption and claimed that it was cooperating with law enforcement officials, Walmart stock fell sharply when the news broke.

These types of issues emphasize the importance of understanding the risks and impacts of company policies, production procedures, and facility oversight worldwide. Following a robust plan and process to identify such issues can save crucial time and dollars in the pursuit of quality performance. The organization needs to develop a method to prioritize the most significant of these aspects and to identify how they impact stakeholders. One method suggested by William Blackburn (2007, p. 704) is outlined in figure 11.2 below:

PRIORITIZATION TOOL FOR SUSTAINABILITY ASPECTS FOR SMS PLANNING

Rating Scale:
1 = Top Rating, Very Important, to Greatest Extent
5 = Lowest Rating, Not Important, to Least Extent

PRIORITY RATINGS

a. Sustainability Aspect	b. Importance to Business Success	c. Importance to Management	d. Consistent with Company Culture	e. Public Visibility or Topic/External Pressure to Act	f. Responsive to Sustainability Trends	g. Extent of Potential Impact	h. Ease of Implementation ($, Time)	I. Overall Priority

Figure 11.2: Prioritizing Sustainability Aspects
(Adapted from Blackburn, 2007, p. 704)

Legal and Other Requirements: The floor and bottom line of compliance for any company are the set of legal requirements applicable to that company's environmental and social aspects. These must be identified at both the local and the international level. Such requirements will also include agreements with customers, suppliers, and codes of conduct. Further, they may include voluntary labeling, trade association rules, or other NGO agreements or guidelines (ISO, 2004, p. 13).

Objectives and Targets: Any objectives or targets should be specific. They must also be measurable and practical. Using the GRI indicators may assist the company with this process. The Baldrige Criteria can also be valuable in helping to identify and ask the right questions and to formulate appropriate indicators apart from the usual financial information.

The objectives should include appropriate planning, design, marketing, and disposal factors. The program outline should include how the company's objectives and targets for each area will be achieved, including suitable timelines, in addition to the applicable resources and personnel needed to implement the plan. These of course can be divided into various different elements of the company's operations. Each division will develop its own plan, and it will flow to the upper-level management for approval and implementation (ISO, 2004, p. 13).

Do (Implementation)

Resources, Roles, and Responsibilities: Successful implementation of the SMS requires a full commitment from the organization, especially at the highest levels. Accordingly, specific officers should be empowered with the authority to oversee the SMS implementation and be given specific responsibilities in this regard. For a large organization, this may involve several people (ISO, 2004, p. 14).

> **Second:**
> **DO**
> Implement your plan
> * Resources, roles and responsibilities
> * Competence, training and awareness
> * Communication
> * Documentation and control of documents
> * Operational controls
> * Emergency preparedness and response

Unilever, for example, has sixty-five "sustainability champions" leading their efforts around the world. In the 1990s, they began integrating sustainability measurements into their manufacturing and sourcing. In 2005, they began to integrate sustainability into each of their brands using their own Brand Imprint tool, developed to provide a 360-degree view of the social, environmental, and economic impacts of each of their products (Unilever, 2012).

You can see that Unilever, one of the world's leading companies in sustainability, is taking this issue seriously. This kind of commitment is needed to make an SMS successful. Adequate resources, including more than just people, need to be allocated to the implementation. This may include buildings, underground tanks, new drainage facilities, purification plants, or even a redesign of an entire product manufacturing process. Communication of the roles and responsibilities for the implementation is key and that message must be spread to all who work for or represent the organization (ISO, 2004, p. 14).

Competence, Training, and Awareness: For implementation to succeed, the company must make sure that it understands the competencies and the talents of its current staff and knows whether or not training is needed. In addition, the company needs to ensure that everyone is aware of the sustainability policy and the SMS, and that every employee understands how those systems will affect their individual position and work (ISO, 2004, p. 14).

The SMS should be a part of what every employee thinks about every day. Each person should be given an opportunity to improve the company's sustainability performance. As stated before, the people on the floor or in the office pool are sometimes closest to the problems, and people are much more likely to implement their own ideas than simply being told what to do.

Communication: Internal communication is vital to the success of the SMS. Messages about its progress can be included in regular company communication features such as staff meetings, intranet sites, blogs, newsletters, tweets, and even old-fashioned signage.

Communication with outside stakeholders should also be formalized and documented regularly. Many companies already have procedures for responding to customers or other stakeholders. These procedures should include relevant portions of the SMS. Any policies for communicating with public authorities in an emergency should also be included in these procedures (ISO, 2004, pp. 14-15).

Documentation and Document Control: Documentation can vary according to the size of the company and its organization. No specific manuals are required, but some sort of regular and consistent documentation should be available to inform those involved in the implementation as well as to provide direction about specific operations. Some examples include the SMS policy itself, the objectives and targets set in the planning stages, information about the significant social and environmental aspects, organizational charts and procedures for implementation, process information about products and services, internal and external standards or regulations, and emergency plans for each site.

Documents should be controlled in a reasonable manner to facilitate implementation and security. The focus should be on performance and not on some involved or overly complex control system (ISO, 2004, pp. 15-16).

Operational Controls: Operational controls sounds like a very boring topic, but these controls are highly important to securing the consistency of production and service delivery. The operation of certain equipment may necessitate specific health and safety concerns. Providing specific instructions on how to operate machinery can be very important (ISO, 2004, p. 16).

What if several people on a particular production line are sick one day? How will the company ensure that the proper processes and procedures are followed? This can also apply to the service industry. Having clear operational procedures and controls will help to ensure that customers are handled efficiently and effectively regardless of the situation. Ensuring that the agreed-upon goals for social and environmental improvement are implemented is highly dependent on the presence of clear operational work instructions and procedures.

Emergency Preparedness and Response: It is necessary for every company to have an emergency plan, with procedures not only for evacuation and safety but also for operation or alternate production procedures should a particular plant be temporarily taken out of operation. The nature of the plan will depend, of course, on the company and its own circumstances, but the types of scenarios to plan for include any on site hazards, storage tanks, or compressed gas, as well as what to do in the event of an explosion or a spill.

Plans should include the most likely types of situations and suggested response. Communication procedures should be included as well. In the event of an emergency, how should management respond internally and how should the public be addressed? Who will be responsible for making any public statements?

Emergency plans should also include recommendations for mitigating and responding to environmental or social injury and how to implement any post-accident evaluation and corrective or preventative procedures. The documentation might even include plans for partnering with neighboring organizations or companies to facilitate a necessary response.

Finally, periodic testing and training is required. The emergency plan must include a list of key personnel to contact, such as the fire department or spillage cleanup companies. Evacuation routes and meeting points should be predetermined. All of this is best managed during the calm of a sunny day, not when disaster strikes.

Check

Monitoring and Measurement: We've talked about documents and operational controls. This is different. Monitoring and measurement means tracking progress according to the goals and targets that were set in the planning stage. This is the actual data collected concerning the social and environmental aspects that were selected for improvement. Documents and operational controls cover what's going on right now and in the future. Records capture what has already happened.

> Third:
> ## CHECK
> Was the plan correct?
> Did you implement it well?
> - Monitoring & measurement
> - Evaluation of compliance
> - Nonconformity, corrective action & preventative action
> - Control of records & internal audit

Keeping regular records of data and tracking trends can inform those implementing the SMS of any patterns that may have appeared. Are they making progress? Do adjustments need to be made to improve results? Have they learned anything new that can lead to even better results and preventative actions (ISO 2004, p. 17)?

Evaluation of Compliance: The planning section began with listing the regulations and legal requirements. In this stage, the company should be able to show that it indeed complied with any applicable laws or regulations.

Nonconformity, Corrective Action, and Preventative Action: Nonconformance means that you didn't meet your goal or that a requirement wasn't implemented properly. This is where you realize that you didn't do what you thought you were going to do, and it needs to be corrected. What was the cause of the problem? How can it be prevented from happening again? Who or what was responsible for making sure it happen in the first place?

There may be an easy fix or the issue may require a more comprehensive, long-term solution. Regardless, corrective action is a very important element of the check phase. The organization must prevent the problem from continuing and find out how to prevent it from happening again. This will move the company forward in pursuit of continuous improvement (ISO, 2004, p. 17).

Records Control and Internal Audits: Records include a multitude of documents such as complaints, training documents, inspection and monitoring reports, management review results, minutes from meetings of stakeholders regarding environmental and social concerns, legal compliance documentation, as well as various communications with interested stakeholders.

Auditing these records—as well as the SMS itself—is part of how the company finds out whether its plans and implementation have succeeded. Audits can take place at different times and places around the company. They constitute an ongoing process, one that ultimately gives management the tools to evaluate the SMS and progress made toward set goals. Audits can be performed by internal personnel or by an external consultant, but the key is to make sure that the auditor is in a position to evaluate the system in an impartial and objective manner.

Act

Management Review: This is the final stage of the plan-do-check-act system and this is where management has the opportunity to review the entire scope and progress of the SMS. Not all aspects need to be reviewed at once. Part of the beauty of the plan-do-check-act

> **Fourth:**
> ## ACT
> Make appropriate adjustments based upon your findings
> • Management review
> • Continual improvement

system is that portions that are progressing more quickly can be implemented, checked, reviewed, and adjusted whenever necessary. Management is able to act, making adjustments and recommendations after the results of the implementation (doing) and evaluation (checking) are complete (ISO, 2004, p. 18).

This is worth saying twice: management doesn't have to wait for the entire company's SMS to be complete in order for it to begin reviewing certain stages and moving forward with new targets and goals for continuous improvement. This is a very important opportunity for the success of the SMS. Engaging in constructive discussion early on when problems are occurring or where surprising success has occurred helps to keep the SMS fluid and vibrant. This also keeps employees engaged in the process.

Finally, after the management review process is complete, new goals and targets may be set, raising the bar for performance and reallocating resources that may have been saved as a result of the SMS process.

Concluding Thoughts

Many companies that tout their own sustainability programs may not have incorporated the ideas contained in this chapter. They may have undertaken a series of initiatives in an effort to remedy what they feel are the most important aspects of their operations with respect to environmental or societal impacts. These companies may emphasize their energy efficiency improvements, their carbon dioxide emission reductions, their reduction in toxic chemicals, or even their use of "all natural" ingredients. This is admirable, but such programs fall well short of what can be accomplished through the incorporation of an SMS fully integrated into the company's existing systems.

Every company has a management system of some sort. By incorporating sustainability into that management system and using the plan-do-check-act framework, the company can make these initiatives operational throughout the organization.

Planning and implementing an SMS takes time. It can take up to eighteen months to plan, implement, and track the improvements described in this chapter. But the payoff is huge. Companies who have embraced sustainability and who have incorporated it into the fabric of their management systems see results.

A recent joint report from MIT and the Boston Consulting Group chronicles a group of companies that are highly committed to sustainability and are profiting from it. Referred to as the "Harvesters," these companies are benefitting in a number of ways, as described in this excerpt (MIT & BCG, 2012, p. 8):

> Some Harvesters are looking at sustainability as a source of innovation, increased market share, and improved profit margins. "Before, it was more about the environment because that's where the leading indicators were in addressing sustainability," says Kimberly-Clark's Ward. "And for us now, it's about looking at

the full spectrum of sustainability." Andreas Regnell, head of strategy and environment for Vattenfall, one of Europe's leading energy companies, says that sustainability "allows us to continue to profit and grow, it helps us to be a responsible business, and it is crucial for our competitive advantage."

Regnell's comment highlights the strength of competitive advantage as a sustainability driver. Having a commitment, a business case, and an ethical stance are important. But commitments can falter, execution can fail, and belief can be supplanted. The reality is that an organization's sustainability agenda often becomes deeply embedded in business processes when it adds to profitability over time.

The plan-do-check-act structure described here can make that embedded quality possible and that structure can be enriched by elements from various international standards or performance frameworks. In fact, the annex of ISO 14001 contains a chart that shows corresponding sections of ISO 14001 and ISO 9001 (quality management). This makes it relatively easy for a company to improve its quality performance while taking on ISO 14001.

The Baldrige Criteria for quality could also be incorporated into the SMS as well as those international standards previously mentioned: ISO 31000 (risk management), ISO 26000 (guidance on social responsibility), ISO 51000 (energy management), and the non-ISO standard OHSAS 1800 (occupational health and safety). Though this may seem like a lot of numbers and labels, each of these standards is replete with ideas and questions to help any company improve its performance, reduce its risk, and move further along a path toward sustainability.

Supplementary Reading Suggestions

For a more extensive look at the Unilever sustainability strategy, view the policy on their website at:
> http://www.unilever.com/sustainable-
> living/ourapproach/oursustainabilitystrategy/.

The ISO 14001 environmental management standard is available for purchase for about $110 US from the ISO website:
> http://www.iso.org/iso/iso14000

There are also free brochures describing this and other ISO standards Drafts and summaries of other ISO standards can be found through a simple Internet search.

References

Blackburn, W. (2007). *The sustainability handbook*. Washington, DC: Environ- mental Law Institute.

International Organization for Standardization (ISO). (2004). *ISO 14001, environmental management systems – requirements with guidance for use*. Geneva: International Organization for Standardization.

International Organization for Standardization (ISO). (2010). *ISO 26000, guidance on social responsibility*. Geneva: International Organization for Standardization.

Kan, M. (2012). Foxconn builds products for many vendors, but its mud sticks to Apple. *Computerworld*. Retrieved from: http://www.computerworld.com/s/article/9232826/Foxconn_builds_products_for_many_vendors_but_its_mud_sticks_to_Apple

Martin, A. (2012). Wal-Mart vows to fix its controls. *New York Times*. Retrieved from: http://www.nytimes.com/2012/04/25/business/wal-mart-says-it-is-tightening-internal-controls.html?_r=0

MIT Sloan Management Review & The Boston Consulting Group (MIT & BCG). (2009). *The business of sustainability*. Cambridge, MA: Massachusetts Institute of Technology. Available from: http://sloanreview.mit.edu/special-report/

MIT Sloan Management Review & The Boston Consulting Group (MIT & BCG). *Sustainability nears a tipping point*. Cambridge, MA: Massachusetts Institute of Technology. Available from: http://sloanreview.mit.edu/special-report/

Unilever. (2012). Our sustainability strategy. Retrieved Oct. 20, 2012 from: http://www.unilever.com/sustainable-living/ourapproach/oursustainabilitystrategy/

Chapter 12

Supply Chain Management

Nestlé believes that it is only by creating value for society and share-holders at the same time that we can have long-term business success. We call this Creating Shared Value. After analyzing our value chain, we have determined that the areas of greatest potential for joint value optimization with society are water, rural development, and nutrition. By working closely with our supply base of 540,000 farmers, we can help them be more productive and emerge from poverty. In return, we receive a higher quality end product, which benefits the consumer and ultimately our business. We commend this approach to other companies and hope this new guide will help spread best practice.
— *Peter Brabeck-Letmathe, Chairman of the Board, Nestlé SA*

Introduction

In today's business parlance, the supply chain is often referred to as the *value chain*. This concept became part of business school training after the publication of Michael Porter's landmark book *The Competitive Advantage* (referred to in Chapter 4). From a facility perspective, the value chain concerns the series of activities and processes performed by a business in order to produce its particular product or service.

From an industry standpoint, the value chain can be expanded to look upstream and downstream from the company itself. What resources are used and how are they extracted or produced? What kinds of human or social impacts are involved in that process and what are the environmental impacts? Is it carbon intensive or water intensive? How secure is the supply stream? Will production be impacted by climate change or population pressure?

After the product or service is produced, what are the downstream impacts? Does the company manufacture a product that uses a lot of energy, such as large transport trucks or airplanes? How is it distributed and delivered? Do customers responsibly dispose of their products, such as soda cans, cell phones, or even prescription drugs or toxic cleaners? How much responsibility does a company have for the use and disposal of its products? These types of questions are more and more becoming an important part of corporate responsibility.

Traceability is also a common concern. If you are a food producer, can you trace where your raw materials were produced? If a contamination problem or an animal welfare issue arose, could you identify whether or not your suppliers were complicit? McDonald's has been a leader in this area, helping to raise the bar for humane animal treatment while also leading the effort for a moratorium on purchases of soybeans from deforested areas in the Amazon.

Some of the big companies that we love to hate are responding to consumer and NGO pressure by providing real leadership in the supply chain of their products. Walmart has been recognized for its efforts to reduce packaging and improve the carbon dioxide footprint of its supply chain, although it remains a target for their social welfare policies. Walmart is pursuing footprint reductions largely because doing so saves them money. Reducing the amount of packaging allows them to put more products on the shelf. More products on the shelf means more products to sell.

Other companies are looking at the supply chain from a resource reliability perspective. Nestlé, for example, implemented a "shared value" program with its cocoa producers, helping them to improve their farming practices and to eliminate some of the supply chain intermediaries in order to ensure fair pricing to farmers and a reliable source of cocoa. Starbucks, after pressure from its customers in the 1990s, developed a cooperative program with coffee producers to ensure their own reliable supply. Doing so enhanced their reputation through their support to coffee farmers.

Companies who approach their supply chain as a value chain from the perspective of all three areas of responsibility (environmental, social, and economic) can distinguish themselves from their competitors and create real, lasting value for their stakeholders. In this chapter, we'll look at how leading companies in this field have accomplished value chain enhancements.

The Sustainable Supply Chain

The supply chain has increasingly become a focus of value creation and not just through compliance or risk management. To reflect on discussions from the last chapter regarding an SMS, the process of making a supply chain more sustainable involves integrating sustainability into *all* aspects of supply chain operations—from sourcing materials to product design and manufacturing, to delivery and distribution, and finally to end of life reclaiming, reuse, or recycling.

As with an SMS, improving the sustainability of a supply chain takes planning, setting goals and priorities, engaging with stakeholders, assigning people and resources to the task, tracking progress, and communicating performance. It becomes its own plan-do-check-act cycle, one that is applied to the entire supply chain.

Several white papers and guides outline these steps and provide examples of companies that have implemented supply chain improvements with notable success. Resources are noted in the suggested reading section at the end of this chapter. Highlights of these tools will be outlined here. For those interested in a deeper look, the suggested documents provide further analysis.

But it's So Complex!

Some companies argue that analyzing their supply chain is simply too complex. This is certainly a concern, but companies working together have been able to manage the multiple data points and to improve performance across the board. Nike, for example, has learned from its past transgressions regarding sweatshop charges in the 1990s. The company is now working in partnership with other apparel manufacturers to improve factory conditions in all of its facilities. Nike has also developed a system to track water quality and efficiency and the company has shared their results with other companies. Nike's new program to eliminate toxins from its products involves partnerships and training programs with various suppliers. It has a goal of zero hazardous chemical discharges across its value chain by 2020 (Greden & Masero, 2012).

In addition to the multitude of data points, some suppliers object to sharing their data, claiming proprietary concerns, or worse yet, ignorance as to the makeup of their products. Ray Anderson complained of this when his suppliers were asked about chemicals used in fabric dyes and fiber processing (Anderson, 2009, p. 73). This can certainly be a problem and a headache, but for Ray at least, persistence paid off. With appropriate stakeholder engagement, he was able to get the information he needed and his suppliers began to see the benefits of working together to improve the footprint of all of the companies along the supply chain.

Developing a standardized format for reporting across the value chain can help to control the variety and quantity of data. Use of appropriate software can help to organize and identify any data anomalies. Some of the common areas to be identified are included in table 12.1 below:

Table 12.1: Key Supply Chain Sustainability Indicators
(Greden & Masero, 2012, p. 9)

Quantitative	Qualitative
Electricity and fuel usage, including renewables	Sustainability product descriptions
Water consumption	Carbon disclosure project participation
Waste disposal – hazardous and non-hazardous	Continuous improvement ideas
Greenhouse gas emissions, scope 1 and 2	Pubic declaration of targets
Restricted substance usage	Community development activities
Reported health and safety incidents	Ethical labor policy

The best way to approach a complex problem is to map it out. Starting with an LCA can be very helpful and there may be several LCAs depending on the multitude of products or services involved. Making sure that this analysis includes social and economic impacts may mean supplementing the analysis with additional information.

Groups and divisions can help to break this process down. Thinking about the *context* of some of the sourcing may be an important ingredient in the analysis as well. Where is the energy coming from (coal-fired plants or renewable energy sources)? Where is the water coming from (an area where water is plentiful or scarce)? What are the working conditions in the various factories or where resources are extracted (are there conflict minerals involved or rare earth minerals)? How are the products recycled (are they sent overseas where recycling may be performed under hazardous conditions)? Making assumptions and creating priorities are a part of any LCA. Understanding those priorities up front can help a company to make better use of the results and to avoid overlooking any important areas.

Connect with Vision and Corporate Objectives

Once you have an overall concept of the supply chain and its impacts, it's time to begin developing an action plan. This includes establishing a business case for the supply chain review. What are the overall benefits to the company from a business standpoint? Are there particular risks to the company's reputation due to resource reliability or labor laws in other countries? Are there efficiencies in transport or delivery that could reduce cost? Is the market changing, or are innovations in product design or delivery required?

Next, establish a clear vision and a list of objectives based on the supply chain sustainability needs. What particular goals and objectives need to be satisfied? Are there certain areas of the supply chain that are most vulnerable or sensitive to the brand's health or to market pressure and that must therefore be pursued first? Clear expectations and goals will help to drive a successful planning process.

Codes of Conduct

Codes of conduct are widely used and may provide a critical tool to establish clear guidelines for suppliers and customers, especially across international boundaries. At minimum, legal requirements should be met, but this is also an opportunity to expand the guidelines to include the company's sustainability vision and goals for environmental and social concerns.

International standards can be used to assist a company in drafting a code of conduct. The ten principles of the Global Compact are a good place to start. These include principles supporting human rights, labor, the environment, and anti-corruption. ISO 26000 (guidance on social responsibility), ISO 14001 (environmental management), OHSAS 18001 (occupational health and safety), and AS 8000 (good governance principles) can all be helpful when drafting a code of conduct.

Engaging with suppliers and benchmarking against other companies can provide an invaluable means to make sure that a code of conduct is complete and reflects the needs of all involved. Should the code be adopted by the suppliers of the suppliers? How far down the tier of influence can you go? This may take time and will depend on the size of the company, but working together with suppliers may enable policy to reach further than originally anticipated.

Levi Strauss was the first multinational company to establish comprehensive global sourcing and operating guidelines. These guidelines were written in two parts. The first part, the Business Partner Terms of Engagement, controls particular issues that are within the control of Levi Strauss and its business partners. The second part, the Country Assessment Guidelines, addresses larger issues extending beyond their partners' direct control, such as political, economic, or social conditions of a particular country. These guidelines help to tackle the choices and risks of doing business in one country versus another (UNGC & BSR, 2010, p. 23).

Determine the Scope

This step seems a bit out of order given how we've discussed scope and footprint so far in relation to the SMS but it makes sense that after the previous planning steps have been completed, it might be helpful to step back and consider how far to push the supply chain management. How far up and down should one go? It may be more effective to begin where stakeholder engagement has already secured an area of trust and to build on that trust. Then, as time goes on, as secure footing has been established, you can branch out along the value chain.

There may be particular hot spots that need attention or a particular event that spurred such ideas in the first place. Or, there may be key suppliers who are critical to the supply chain and to the company's survival. Start there.

Eventually, it may become important to look further down the supply chain spectrum. Ford Motor Company, for example, goes so far as to take action regarding the production of pig iron, which is six or seven tiers down their supply chain. But pig iron is used to make steel and Ford uses a lot of steel. It's a good move for them.

Overall, as a company becomes more experienced and more capable in dealings with its suppliers, it can expand the scope of its supply chain engagement (UNGC & BSR, 2010, p. 25).

Align and Implement

Aligning the goals of the company and engaging with suppliers enables implementation of supply chain improvements to be performed more efficiently. This is where the rubber meets the road, so to speak. Implementation may include helping certain suppliers to build their capabilities and then auditing their results. This can range from factory training to teaching farmers how to improve their production techniques or even supplying tools or more efficient irrigation infrastructure.

Hewlett-Packard (HP), for example, initiated a worker training program that included cooperation with a local NGO to ensure that electronic codes of conduct were met in the factories of two of its suppliers (codes according to the Electronic Industry Citizenship Coalition). The training included workers' rights awareness, creating worker hot lines and training workers on how to oversee them, resolving various labor issues, and developing counseling and communication programs (UNGC & BSR, 2010, p. 38).

Nestlé's shared value program with cocoa farmers includes working with NGOs and the governments of Ghana and Côte d'Ivoire to prevent child labor on cocoa farms and to improve farming techniques. They have reduced the number of intermediaries in the supply chain to improve control and to ensure that cocoa farmers get a fair price for their products (UNGC & BSR, 2010, p. 40).

Tracking Performance and Communication

As with the plan-do-check-act cycle for an SMS, the last stages for supply chain management involve tracking progress, assessing performance, and communicating recommended revisions and modifications.

Further, signatories to the Global Compact are required to report to their suppliers on their progress toward implementation of the ten principles. Overall, sustainability reporting offers opportunities for companies to not only clarify their sustainability goals but also to communicate their progress to important stakeholders. Reports can become a source of best practices, setting examples for suppliers, as well as a chance to track continuous improvement for the organization. Setting goals and reporting on them can also encourage accountability within the organization, a positive for those involved as stated goals are achieved (UNGC & BSR, 2010, p. 62).

Shared Value

The concept of shared value was first explored in an article by Michael Porter and Robert Kramer in 2006. They proclaimed that corporations were missing an opportunity to attain a competitive advantage by ignoring important social investments. They framed these corporate social responsibility measures as a way to strengthen opportunities for advancement versus just a charitable handout or a means to control risk (Porter & Kramer, 2006).

By 2011, Porter and Kramer had crystallized their thoughts into the concept of *shared value,* and in their groundbreaking article published in the *Harvard Business Review,* they have now firmly established their footing in the sustainability arena. Shared value is described as the connection between business success and social progress. It means creating economic value for a company that also creates social value for those involved in its processes or influence. Both benefit from this connection.

By connecting economic benefit and social benefit, Porter and Kramer argue that a company goes beyond philanthropy or corporate social responsibility—or even sustainability. This connection puts social progress at the center of what a business needs to succeed, for it cannot succeed in the long term by ignoring resource depletion or outsourcing production to countries with lower wages. The solution, they argue, is to create innovation and growth through partnerships with the communities in which they operate (Porter & Kramer, 2011, p. 62). Shared value is seen as the natural progression from philanthropy to corporate social responsibility to corporate shared value. Figure 12.1 below illustrates this progression.

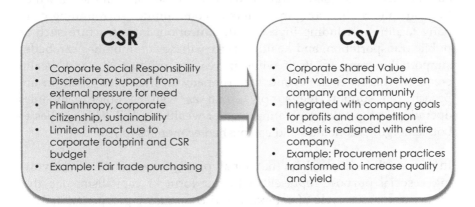

Figure 12.1: From Corporate Social Responsibility to Corporate Shared Value
(Porter & Kramer, 2011, p. 76)

The concept is only now beginning to be tested in the market, but the list of major companies that are embracing this approach is impressive. Besides Nestlé, the list includes Google, IBM, Walmart, Unilever, Johnson & Johnson, and Intel (p. 63).

Shared value is not a handout or a redistribution of wealth. Rather, it is an expansion of the pool of wealth that is controlled by both the company and the society affected. For example, the fair trade coffee concept is closer to a redistribution of wealth. It establishes a guaranteed price for farmers for their goods, thereby increasing their income while guaranteeing product for the company. Shared value means investing in the local cluster of farming communities to improve their practices to reduce impacts on the land, increase revenue by improved quality and yields, and improve efficiency in market transactions. This benefits the company by guaranteeing a higher quality supply and reducing transaction costs. Porter and Kramer report that initial studies of shared value have shown that farmers in the Côte d'Ivoire increased their incomes by more than a factor of ten. Fair trade increased income by 10 to 20 percent whereas shared value increased their income by over 300 percent (p. 68).

Porter and Kramer view shared value as the next logical step in the evolution of capitalism. They emphasize that this is a business decision rooted in creating real, lasting value for a company—a key to unlocking new waves of innovation and growth (p. 77). Companies today complain about a lack of adequately trained workers in the communities in which they operate. By investing in clusters of communities surrounding company facilities, including investing in education, infrastructure such as public transportation, and health services, these communities can better support the company itself while increasing productivity and wealth creation. This extends beyond the company in multiples. Such an approach can support the supply chain as well as other companies operating in the area, generating greater wealth overall. This applies to both emerging economies and established economies (p.73).

In essence, the authors claim that not all profits are equal. "Profits involving a social purpose represent a higher form of capitalism, one that creates a positive cycle of company and community prosperity" (p. 76). They admit that not all social problems can be resolved through this concept. However, this approach does offer an opportunity for corporations to perform a leadership role in a way that neither governments nor NGOs have the capability, the capital, or the resources to undertake. The power of corporate energy and assets can be harnessed to tackle problems in innovative and creative ways. This is an encouraging concept.

Concluding Thoughts

Engaging with a company's supply chain presents an opportunity to extend the company's own sustainability initiatives beyond its direct sphere of influence. Working with customers, suppliers, suppliers of suppliers, and beyond, an organization can extend their reach, creating significant impact beyond the property line of the factory or company headquarters.

In addition, working with stakeholders in the supply chain means that you don't have to go it alone. Forming partnerships and alliances in this area result in more like minds working together, uncovering new opportunities, sharing innovation, and opening new markets.

Supply chain management doesn't have to happen all at once. It can begin with a key supplier or one trusted partner. Working from that foundation, supply chain engagement can spread, progressing to many stages of influence.

Many companies are already using these tools to create more responsible sourcing of materials, more efficient use of products, and better treatment of employees around the world. Those mentioned here represent only a few of the growing number who have embraced the value chain and are using it to improve their own performance, credibility, and profitability.

Supplementary Reading Suggestions

The United Nations Global Compact and Business for Social Responsibility (BSR) have published an excellent guide on supply chain sustainability, which includes step-by-step instructions on how to implement a successful program. It contains many examples from companies who have tackled this issue and describes the benefits they have obtained from supply chain engagement.

> UN Global Compact Office and Business for Social Responsibility (UNGC & BSR). (2010). *Supply chain sustainability: a practical guide for continuous improvement.* Available for free download from: http://supply-chain.unglobalcompact.org/site/article/68

Two other helpful guides include the following:

> Greden, L, Masero, S. (2012). Accelerate sustainability results with visibility and accountability across the value chain. CA Technologies. Available for free download from:
> http://research.environmentalleader.com/content19892

> New Zealand Business Council for Sustainable Development. (2003). *Business guide to a sustainable supply chain, a practical guide.* New Zealand Business Council for Sustainable Development. Available for free download from:
> http://www.commdev.org/business-guide-sustainable-supply-chain-practical-guide

Finally, I highly recommended reading Michael Porter and Mark Kaplan's *Harvard Business Review* article on shared value. You can read it online at the HBR website (http://hbr.org/2011/01/the-big-idea-creating-shared-value). Though you will most likely have to purchase the article to view it in full, it is well worth the read, especially for anyone interested in learning more about this subject:

Porter, M.E. & Kramer, M.R. (2011). Creating shared value: how to reinvent capitalism – and unleash a wave of innovation and growth. *Harvard Business Review*. Available at:
http://hbr.org/2011/01/the-big-idea-creating-shared-value

For a free teaser, you can also watch Michael Porter explain the concept of share value and describe his excitement regarding how businesses can drive real societal and environmental change through shared value in the future:
http://www.youtube.com/watch?v=s7i4FrkUK4g&feature=relmfu

References

Anderson, R.C. (2009). *Confessions of a radical industrialist: profits, people, purpose – doing business by respecting the earth.* New York: St. Martin's Press.

Goldberg, R.A. & Yagen, J.D. (2007). McDonald's corporation: managing a sustainable supply chain. Harvard Business School Publishing. Retrieved from: http://www.hbsp.harvard.edu

Greden, L, Masero, S. (2012). Accelerate sustainability results with visibility and accountability across the value chain. CA Technologies. Retrieved from: http://research.environmentalleader.com/content19892

Porter, M.E. & Kramer, M.R. (2006). Strategy and society: the link between competitive advantage and corporate social responsibility. *Harvard Business Review, 84*(12), 78-92.

Porter, M.E. & Kramer, M.R. (2011). Creating shared value: how to reinvent capitalism – and unleash a wave of innovation and growth. *Harvard Business Review, 89*(1/2), 62-77.

UN Global Compact Office and Business for Social Responsibility (UNGC & BSR). (2010). Supply chain sustainability: a practical guide for continuous improvement. Retrieved from: http://supply-chain.unglobalcompact.org/site/article/68

Chapter 13

Sustainability Metrics

Always focus on the front windshield and not the review mirror.
— Colin Powell

Introduction

In today's world, it can seem that we are awash in data. Reports and analyses on the economy, job growth, carbon dioxide emissions, water pollution, and population growth are only a few clicks away. News about a company's performance, or lack thereof, can spread like wildfire over the news channels and across social media websites.

Making sense of the mountains of data available and reporting on that data will be the subject of the next two chapters. In this chapter, we'll investigate how to pick appropriate indicators for the goals selected to achieve corporate progress. In the next, we'll take a look at how to report on those goals in a meaningful and comprehensive manner.

How can you describe a company's goals and objectives such that they can be adequately tracked and measured? Doing so is often a two-way process. The goals may be need to be modified to allow for accurate tracking. If they are too broad or too vague, there may be no way to know whether or not they can be achieved.

Setting goals that are specific, measurable, achievable, relevant, and timely (or SMART) allows them to be tracked by the company and even linked to compensation or bonuses as a means to provide accountability. Framing these goals in a positive light makes them aspirational— something that everybody in the company can get excited about and rally around. These goals will be met with more success than those cast in a negative tone. Framing them as such can be easier said than done, however, and many companies struggle with connecting goals to indicators in a meaningful and successful way. But by planning ahead and thinking carefully about the connections between goals and metrics, companies can make sure their hard work is not wasted (Blackburn, 2007, pp. 225-227).

Materiality

When thinking about what metrics to choose, companies must first consider the materiality of those metrics. Doing so will help to reduce the flood of data to a more focused and manageable data set, one that is both more relevant and more meaningful.

Materiality has been approached from a number of angles in the sustainability field. The GRI guidelines define materiality as information that reflects the significant environmental, social, and economic impacts of the organization or those that would "substantively influence" the decisions and assessments of its stakeholders (GRI, 2000-2011, p. 8). But what is "significant," and how do you decide what would substantively influence stakeholder decisions?

GRI explains that the opinions of established experts in the field can serve as a reference for these decisions. LCA and impact assessment methodologies can be used to help define these areas. In addition, any area that has already been selected for active management by the organization would be considered material (GRI, 2000-2011, p. 8).

Another way to look at materiality comes from the Global Environmental Management Initiative (GEMI), which published a guide on metrics in which they suggest using the following four criteria to assess materiality (GEMI, 2007, p. 10):

- Relevance to the business strategy
- Significance of the organization's environmental, social, and/or economic impacts
- Level of concern to external stakeholders
- Ability of the organization to control or influence

These factors can be analyzed by a group of company representatives including key stakeholder representatives. These issues should be considered both from the *outside in* and from the *inside out*.

From the inside, what are the key risks to the business and how do these risks relate to the significance of the impacts identified? How much control does the company have over these impacts? How do these impacts relate to the overall goals and values of the company?

From the outside, what are the common questions and issues raised by your stakeholders? What are your peers and your competitors addressing? Are there important rules and regulations that apply to your business that need more attention?

By engaging a group to analyze these questions and to identify key areas, a list of the most material issues can be identified (Gardner, 2011, 2012). Figure 13.1 below shows an example from GRI of how materiality can be mapped using this process.

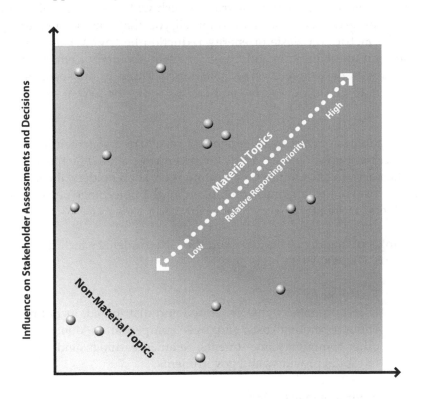

Significance of Economic, Environmental, and Social Impacts

Figure 13.1: Mapping Materiality
(GRI, 2000-2011, p. 8)

By identifying the key material issues for consideration, the company can also make sure to include these issues in their annual report or sustainability report. In fact, by assimilating the frequently asked questions from various stakeholders, including those who are conducting surveys for the field, a company can make sure that those questions are answered in their regular reports (Gardner, 2011). Then, when the survey comes in, they can simply forward their report. Voilà!

Leading and Lagging Indicators

Given that you have now decided on the important areas to measure, you need to identify the appropriate metrics to be used to track those material issues and impacts.

How do you choose the right metrics? Which will give you a real picture of your progress? Do financial results tell you that you are succeeding? Will the metrics on waste or energy reduction be key? What about the efforts put into education and training? What about your efforts to hire local experts or a more diverse labor force? Those in the sustainability field love to talk about *lagging* and *leading* indicators. What exactly are they?

Lagging indicators are measurements of results or a statement reflective of the current position, such as the net revenue generated by the business for the past year, the return on investment for shareholders, the percentage of waste reduction for a certain plant, or the percentage of work days lost due to accidents or injury on the job.

Examples of lagging indicators from the GRI guidelines include the following (GRI, 2000-2011):

> Economic (p. 26):
> Direct economic value generated and distributed, including revenues, operating costs, employee compensation, donations, and other community investments, retained earnings, and payments to capital providers and governments.

> Environmental (p. 28):
> Percentage of materials used that are recycled input materials.

Social (p. 31):
Rates of injury, occupational diseases, lost days, and absenteeism, and total number of work-related fatalities, by region and
by gender.

Leading indicators are measurements of efforts made to improve performance, such as education and training. They can include surveys
measuring attitudes or behaviors or even sensitivity to a local license to
operate. Leading indicators tend to be more qualitative than quantitative,
but they also will be more predictive of future performance versus simply a measurement of past performance results.

Investing in education and training leads to a work force that is better
prepared and that can be promoted from within the company. This saves
money and time, since new hires are generally less productive until they
become familiar with their jobs and the company goals and structure. As
mentioned in Chapter 10, time spent planning can greatly increase
productivity and reduce the amount of time wasted by those who don't
understand the goals and direction of the company.

Some examples of leading indicators from GRI include (GRI, 2000-2011):

Economic (p. 26):
Development and impact of infrastructure investments and services provided primarily for public benefit through commercial,
in-kind, or pro bono engagement.

Environment (p. 28):
Strategies, current actions, and future plans for managing impacts on biodiversity.

Social (p. 35):
Total hours of employee training on policies and procedures
concerning aspects of human rights that are relevant to operations, including the percentage of employees trained.

Some argue that lagging indicators merely tell you where you have been
and therefore cannot tell you where you are going. (Colin Powell is most
likely not a fan of lagging indicators.) However, *trends* of lagging indicators (results of performance) can at least give you an idea of the direction
in which you are headed. At the same time, trends can't truly tell you

where you'll be in the future. Circumstances can arise that turn those results on a dime. A hurricane could hit your drill rig and set it on fire. A news team could discover oppressive labor practices at one of your factories. An explosion at one of your mines could be found to have been caused by ignored safety standards. But lagging indicators are an important part of the indicator mix. For a complete picture, you need both leading and lagging indicators.

Together, leading and lagging indicators provide a more comprehensive analysis of how a company is performing with respect to its goals. Matching up the indicators with the goals, or even "tweaking" or customizing the indicators to provide a more accurate indication of progress, can help the company to measure progress and communicate that progress to management as well as those in the field.

For example, Procter & Gamble (P&G) has adopted a number of goals to further its vision to improve sustainability through its products. Some of those goals include access to clean water, improved hygiene, and better quality of life for women and children around the world. To measure their progress, P&G introduced "value-created" metrics such as lives saved, disease avoided, and the number of children reaching their full development potential. Working with NGOs in the area, P&G has been able to determine the effect of their water purifiers by measuring the reduction in cases of diarrhea in the region. This can help them determine the effectiveness of their product and the success of its implementation in a given population (GEMI, 2007, p. 38). Using a combination of metrics, P&G can therefore evaluate how it is progressing toward its goals.

Linking Indicators

Linking performance indicators (whether leading or lagging) to financial benefit can strengthen the business case for those goals that the indicators are tracking. What are the savings from the waste reduction program? What is the increased productivity from the training program or from the diversity goals? Tracking some of these gains may not be exact, but even a value estimate may motivate those in the finance department who may not share the same vision as those in the human resources department. Sharing this information across departments can help build support for sustainability programs.

Further, complementary goals can ensure that improvements in one area don't occur at the expense of another area. Improving efficiency in a food production line shouldn't come at the expense of food quality or taste. Using a balanced scorecard in the evaluation and measurement of these types of goals can prevent such trade-offs (Blackburn, 2007, p. 246).

Key Performance Indicators

Finally, developing key performance indicators (KPIs) for the company will help to keep the teams focused and will prevent them from being overwhelmed by the number of data points. KPIs are developed by using the processes described thus far. First, determine what is material to report. Then, connect the top goals from the strategy process with the indicators needed to measure progress on those goals. The result of this process would be a list of KPIs that could be assembled in a company dashboard report to summarize progress on a regular basis. These would include both leading and lagging indicators, of course.

Some examples of industry-wide KPIs for environmental, social, governance, and long-term viability include the following (EFFAS, 2009, p. 5):

Environmental:
- Energy efficiency
- Greenhouse gas emissions

Social:
- Staff turnover
- Training and qualifications
- Maturity of work force
- Absenteeism rate

Governance:
- Litigation risks
- Corruption

Long-term viability:
- Revenues from new products

These are just general KPIs. More specific indicators should be developed that more closely match your particular company. However, the information above does provide guidance regarding the types of indicators that might be included across all areas of the sustainability spectrum. An example of a company dashboard is shown in figure 13.2 below

Johnson&Johnson Environmental Performance Dashboard
(Example)

Next Generation Goal	Progress	Reasons / Comments
Compliance / Risk Management		3 Non-compliance events
Management Systems / ISO 14001		ISO certified, MAARS rating=2, MAP not reviewed and signed, 100% of MAP items on time, CCO plan ongoing & on schedule
New Product / Process Review		100% of New Products/Processes/Packaging reviewed using the DfE tool or equivalent
External Manufacturing		76% EM with EHS contract language, 40% EM audits on schedule, 100% EM audited before use. 0 unacceptable EM, 0 Marginal EM
Energy Use		93% Enhanced Best Practices implemented
Water Use		81% Best practices implemented. Cumulative PBA = 7.15, Water Usage = 502,386m^3, Avoided = 35,897m^3
Raw Material Use		Total avoidance: 1,589,456 Total usage: 53,165,445 (PBA: 3.0)
Packaging Use		Packaging avoidance = 725,489 Packaging Use - 13,592,000 (5.4 PBA)
Water Reduction (NPO)	1 2 3 4	1. Non-haz NPO avoided = 1,275,194 Total Non-haz NPO = 81,095,432 (1.57 PBA) 2. Haz NPO avoided = 14,146,302 Total Haz NPO = 109,443,578 (12.9 PBA) 3. Toxic NPO avoided = 1. 914,000 Total Toxic NPO = 32,403,396 (5.9 PBA) 4. Use of Preferred Waste Mgmt Method = 16% decrease 2000

Figure 13.2: Johnson & Johnson Company Dashboard
(GEMI, 2007, p. 50)

This type of chart or table gives a quick overview of the progress made toward key goals using simple color coding to show progress.

Concluding Thoughts

Metrics are intended to provide the necessary information to management and other important stakeholders regarding progress made toward the company's goals. They must be clear and understandable, and they should be communicated throughout the company to ensure buy-in from all departments. Visual depictions and graphs can help with these communication efforts. Dashboard summaries provide a quick overview of progress including where more efforts should be concentrated.

Considerations regarding metrics include the ability to combine or "roll up" the metrics from individual departments to provide summaries. At the same time, they should provide detail to those who desire it. Metrics must also be communicated in context. What is the historical basis for the measurement? How has it changed? Is it an absolute measurement (such as absolute greenhouse gas reduction for the company) or is it based upon sales (greenhouse gas per gross sales revenue)?

The results of metrics selection and presentation should be critically analyzed by the organization. Do they serve their purpose? Are they truly supporting the business strategy? Do they help to engage the employees and other important stakeholders? Are they serving to change behavior if that is desired?

Providing this feedback to the management team can result in valuable adjustments and improvements made to the metrics process. Having the right tools to measure success toward the company's sustainability goals will ensure continued progress and improvement (GEMI, 2007, pp. 49-53).

Supplementary Reading Suggestions

GEMI has published an excellent guide to metrics referenced in this chapter. It includes step-by-step instruction for developing goals, metrics, and indicators, as well as instruction for conducting materiality tests. The guide includes many case study examples to better illustrate their points. This guide is available for free download from the GEMI website.

> Global Environment Management Initiative (GEMI). (2007). *The Metrics Navigator*. Washington, DC: Global Environment Management Initiative. Retrieved from:
> http://www.gemi.org/metricsnavigator/.

The European Federation of Financial Analysts Societies (EFFAS) paper referenced in this chapter contains a comprehensive evaluation of KPIs across various sectors and industries. The final version of KPIs for ESG 3.0 (published in 2010) is available for download at the EEFAS website: http://www.effas-esg.com/?p=265.

References

Blackburn, W. (2007). *The sustainability handbook*. Washington, DC: Environ- mental Law Institute.

European Federation of Financial Analysts Societies (EFFAS). (2009). *KPIs for ESG: key performance indicators for environmental, social and governance issues, version 1.2*. Frankfurt: EFFAS.

Gardner, M. (2011). Sustainability survey fatigue? Retrieved from: http://www.sustainserv.com/de/easyblog/entry/sustainability-survey-fatigue.html

Gardner, M. (2012). The relevance of sustainability data: GRI materiality test. Presentation to Harvard University Extension School class, ENVR-E-105 Corporate Sustainability Strategy, Nov. 15, 2012.

Global Environment Management Initiative (GEMI). (2007). *The metrics navigator*. Washington, DC: Global Environment Management Initiative. Retrieved from: http://www.gemi.org/metricsnavigator/

Global Reporting Initiative (GRI). (2000-2011). *RG, sustainability reporting guidelines, version 3.1*. Amsterdam: Global Reporting Initiative.

Chapter 14

Reporting on Sustainability Performance

Not everything that counts can be counted, and not everything that can be counted counts.

—Albert Einstein

Introduction

Over the past two decades, corporate reporting on environmental and social impacts has increased by leaps and bounds. Many managers now understand that you can only manage what you measure. Keeping records of important data points for environmental and social concerns has become as important as collecting financial results. Shareholder proxies focused on these issues have increased dramatically over just the past decade. At many of the larger companies senior management has taken note (Ernst & Young, 2011).

Sustainability reporting has evolved immeasurably over this time period as well. Various reporting frameworks have been developed, including those formulated by GRI and the Carbon Disclosure Project, in addition to AccountAbility's AA1000 standards, and ISO standards such as ISO 14001 (environmental management), ISO 9001 (quality management), and ISO 26000 (guidance on social responsibility).

The GRI guidelines are steadily becoming the most widely accepted standard for reporting. With revisions released every few years following circulation for public comment, GRI's guidelines clearly reflect the workings of an organization seeking to continually improve reporting metrics as well as data analysis and selection for sustainability reporting (Tng, 2010).

How does one decide what to include in a sustainability report? Who is actually going to read it? What kinds of data are important to include and how can you make it relevant to the goals and targets that the company has set for its sustainability journey?

The GRI guidelines offer some advice in this area, but many other scholars and analysts have weighed in on these questions as well. We'll take a look at how they've tackled these questions and more in this chapter.

Financial Reporting

Publicly traded companies in the United States are required to file a number of reports. The SEC requires publicly traded companies to file Form 10-K on an annual basis. This document is usually lengthy and can be arduous to read, but it includes vital information about the company's operating income and expenses, possible risks, opportunities, assets, and liabilities.

Public companies are also required to file a proxy statement, which includes information such as the names and biographies of the directors, salaries of top management, and major issues brought before the shareholders, such as bylaw amendments, company mergers, or spin-offs. Increasingly, shareholder-sponsored proxy resolutions focus on environmental or social issues (Ernst & Young, 2012).

The Sarbanes-Oxley Act of 2002 has also had an impact on corporate financial reporting by requiring management to disclose the internal controls in place regarding financial management. This act holds the company CEO and CFO responsible for the information that is presented, including stiff penalties for noncompliance (Peavler, 2012).

As the risks of environmental and social impacts become more widely recognized by companies, investors, and other stakeholders, the inclusion of these issues in the corporate 10-K and annual reports has increased. These types of issues are no longer relegated just to the company's sustainability or corporate responsibility (CR) report. In fact, some companies and stock exchanges around the world are requiring more public reporting of CR initiatives, including Brazil, Denmark, Sweden, the Netherlands, South Africa, and Malaysia (Boston College, 2009, p. 2).

The trend toward integrated reporting is real. More and more companies are combining their sustainability reports with their annual reports, showing the connections between the various goals and targets, while helping stakeholders to understand their organization's strategic direction.

Trends in Non-financial Reporting

Just as sustainability has evolved tremendously over the past twenty years, so has sustainability reporting—or *non-financial reporting* as it is commonly called in the business community. And, just as sustainability is now being integrated into business organizations, sustainability reporting is becoming a major part of corporate communications.

Companies who are working to improve their sustainability footprint are anxious to spread the word about their accomplishments. Greenwashing is certainly still a danger and companies continue to wrestle with the balance of transparency versus backlash should their information be overstated. But with clear objectives, solid data, and an increase in two-way communication, the sustainability reporting field is maturing to a new level of competency.

A 2011 survey of 250 of the largest global companies found that 95 percent report on corporate responsibility topics compared to 80 percent in the previous survey in 2008. While this makes one think that the tipping point has indeed been reached, it should be noted that European-based companies are clearly leading the way. Two-thirds of the non-reporting companies were based in the United States. US-based reporting is on the rise, however, according to current trends (KPMG, 2011, p. 6).

The leading drivers for CR reporting are reputation, ethical considerations, and employee motivation. Surprisingly, economic considerations have fallen from high on the list of reasons for reporting in 2008 to seventh place. Risk management is also listed as a concern, but by only about 35 percent of responders. Cost savings is listed dead last (KPMG, 2011, p. 19).

At the same time, close to half of the companies surveyed by KPMG stated that they gained financial benefit from their CR initiatives. Brand value, innovation, and consumer recognition were cited as top benefits (KPMG, 2011, p. 19).

Although the number of companies preparing CR reports is on the rise, the quality of that reporting remains mixed. The creation of standards and frameworks is helping, however, and third-party certification as well as auditing of these reports has helped to improve the credibility of the information.

Some companies are truly shining in this area, including Nike, Coca-Cola, Timberland, Ford, Seventh Generation, and General Electric. Combining sustainability information with financial results has enabled these companies to prove that their strategies are working across various departments, driving success throughout their companies.

Reading Sustainability Reports

Who reads sustainability reports anyway? A survey by SustainAbility in 2008 found that 55 percent of responders read these reports for consumer and purchasing reasons. Other responders included 45 percent for investing, 38 percent for engagement, and 32 percent for employment. Also included were business-to-business and partnership affiliations. So there are a variety of audiences who may read sustainability reports; there is therefore a variety of information presented in them.

Sorting through the volume of data and figures included in some reports can be daunting. But analyzing the various sections step by step can help to prevent feeling overwhelmed by a one-hundred-page report.

One key element is a letter from the company CEO. The information included in that letter can be illuminating. Does it provide specific goals or is it just a list of generalities about the company's vision and mission? A more specific list of goals, challenges, and targets met or missed, resources devoted to those targets, and plans to achieve those goals would be both more satisfying and more informative. Is the company a leader in the industry? Are they tying management compensation to targets set? These types of statements can at least provide some hints regarding the seriousness of a company's commitment to sustainability. The mission and vision statement for the company and for its sustainability policies can set the stage for the report, allowing for a better understanding of strategies and goals (Boston College, 2010, p. 24).

Summaries of the key facts and figures for environmental and social goals are an indication that the company understands its progress and can relate that progress to its mission and vision. Summary information may also include a quick overview of the company's most important challenges and accomplishments. Without such a summary, the reader can question whether the company has made the kinds of connections it should between its financial welfare and its impacts on the environment and society (Boston College, 2010, p 26).

If the report includes graphs and tables, are they clear and easy to understand? Do they present data in both absolute as well as normalized figures? Do they map progress against goals from previous years? Can comparisons be made with other companies in the same industry?

These are all questions that would be answered in a well-presented report. Sometimes too much data can be presented, which brings us to the question of materiality—what is material to the reader? This was discussed in the previous chapter on metrics. Companies that simply present a data dump in their reports are doing a disservice to their interested stakeholders. More careful organization of the data according to clear targets and progress toward those goals shows maturity in reporting and direct attention to what is material to report.

Coca-Cola, for example, has well-articulated goals and graphs throughout its award-winning sustainability report for 2010-2011 (more about that award later). Figure 14.1 below shows some of the goals that are highlighted in their section about water, noting that some goals have not been achieved, but outlining the progress they have made.

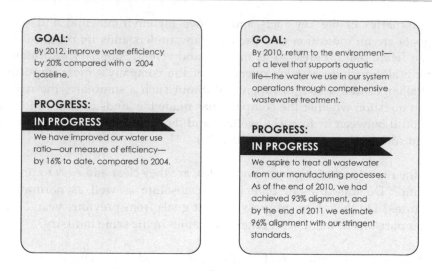

GOAL:
By 2012, improve water efficiency by 20% compared with a 2004 baseline.

PROGRESS:

IN PROGRESS

We have improved our water use ratio—our measure of efficiency—by 16% to date, compared to 2004.

GOAL:
By 2010, return to the environment—at a level that supports aquatic life—the water we use in our system operations through comprehensive wastewater treatment.

PROGRESS:

IN PROGRESS

We aspire to treat all wastewater from our manufacturing processes. As of the end of 2010, we had achieved 93% alignment, and by the end of 2011 we estimate 96% alignment with our stringent standards.

Figure 14.1: Clear Goals and Progress in Coca-Cola Report
(Coca-Cola, 2011, pp. 20-21)

Coca-Cola uses consistent formatting for tables and graphs throughout their report, making it easy to assimilate the information at a glance. Figure 14.2 below shows an example of a graph illustrating their water use ratios from 2004 to 2010 (the goal referred to on the left in figure 14.1 above).

Coca-Cola System Water Use Ratio from 2004 to 2010
Average plant ratios based on collected data (liters/liter of product produced)

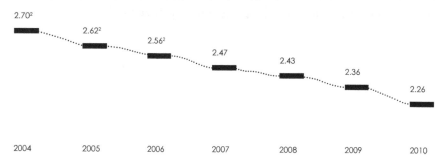

[2]Our water use and water use ratio (efficiency) figures have been recalculated for the Europe Group 2004, 2005 and 2006, based on changes to the organization. These changes affected our system water use for those three years.

Figure 14.2: Graph Example from Coca-Cola Report
(Coca-Cola, 2011, p. 20)

Nike, another award-winner in reporting, created a three-year summary report that covers all aspects of the company, including governance, financial results, overall strategy, environmental impacts, social impacts, and even information concerning political contributions. It's a tome at 176 pages, but the report uses clear and consistent formatting to present goals and charts, making it quite readable and easy to grasp. A sample of one of Nike's goals is shown in figure 14.3 below.

EXCESSIVE OVERTIME TARGET

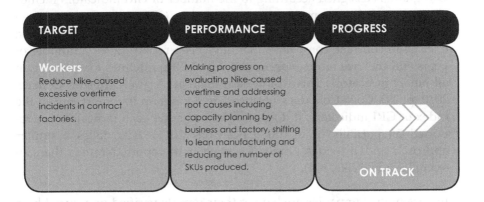

Note: In our FY05/06 report we released a target of zero excessive overtime identified in contract factories. As we started working toward that goal we realized that this goal was measuring the wrong thing. The target of eliminating "identified" overtime could be achieved by incentivizing lower levels of identification and reporting whereas our over arching aim is to increase tracking and transparency. While we seek to reduce excessive overtime across the industry, the only items we can directly influence are those caused by Nike.

Figure 14.3: Goal Example from Nike Report
(Nike, 2009, p. 53)

Nike's report is comprehensive and serves as an example of a "one report" document – including all aspects of the business and attempting to identify the connections between the various financial, environmental and social impacts. This company is obviously taking its responsibilities seriously and has made huge progress since its challenges with the accusations of sweatshop factories in the 1990s.

Companies that are using the GRI framework may include a GRI Index along with their reporting. This can facilitate the location of specific GRI indicators that were reported upon. Although this isn't required by GRI, having such an index shows a level of sophistication by the company doing the reporting (Boston College, 2010, p. 28). Coca-Cola includes such an index at the end of its report, and it also includes a section of "performance highlights" at the end that includes all the goals such as pictured in figure 14.1, and the progress achieved toward those goals (Coca-Cola, 2011). Nike does not include the index on its printed report, but it includes a link in the PDF of the report version to the GRI index posted on its website (Nike, 2007-2009, p. 167).

A GRI grade may also be included. It should be noted that this is a self-assessed grade and not something that is evaluated by GRI. Rather, a GRI grade is assigned according to the number of GRI indicators included in a report. For example, companies new to GRI may include only ten of the possible ninety indicators. Such a company would be graded at a C level. In contrast, companies that have been reporting for a number of years and that are more experienced with GRI guidelines may report on all ninety indicators. This would earn them an A grade (Boston College, 2010, p. 29). Coca-Cola does not provide a grade in its report, but in the index of GRI indicators, it does stipulate whether each indicator was reported on partially or in full (Coca-Cola, 2011). Nike takes a similar approach and provides grades for each item reported rather than an overall grade (Nike, n.d).

Increasingly, companies are having their reports verified or assured by a third party. This can be a source of credibility for the company, but for smaller companies, the expense of an audit may not be possible, a fact that should not be considered detrimental. For larger firms, however, the trend is to hire one of the large accounting firms such as KPMG, Ernst & Young, Deloitte, or Pricewaterhouse Coopers to audit and verify their results (Boston College, 2010, p. 30).

Award-Winning Reports

A number of associations rate companies based on their CR reporting. In the United States, the Ceres–Association of Chartered Certified Accountants (ACCA) awards have become prominent. Formulated in 2002, these awards are presented annually. The winner for 2010 was Nike, who was recognized for its efforts to integrate sustainability into all aspects of its business, including strategic planning, supply chain operations, and product design (Ceres, 2011).

The Ceres-ACCA awards are presented in accordance with the following criteria (Boston College, 2010, p. 65):

- Completeness (40 percent): includes materiality, strategy, stakeholder inclusion, and organizational context
- Credibility (35 percent): includes governance, management processes, performance, stakeholder inclusion, and assurance
- Communications (25 percent): includes presentation, structure, and stakeholder inclusion

A global award program sponsored by CorporateRegister.com is awarded based on votes cast by its thirty-five thousand members (company employees are not allowed to vote for their own company). Coca-Cola Enterprises received the award in 2011 (CorporateRegister.com, 2012). CorporateRegister.com asked those voting to consider the following criteria: content, communication, credibility, commitment, and comparability (Boston College, 2010, p. 65).

Overall, what you should look for in a CR report is whether or not the company is connecting the dots between its environmental and social goals and targets and its financial reporting. The most successful, integrated report will make this connection, which we will discuss at the end of this chapter. A quick review of the Coca-Cola and Nike sustainability reports is a useful exercise after reading this section. What elements have been completed well? Are there any holes that you can see? Links to these reports are available in the supplementary reading section at the end of this chapter.

Preparing Sustainability Reports

There are three leading organizations that provide standards for sustainability reporting today: AccountAbility, GRI, and SustainAbility.

As mentioned previously, the GRI guidelines have become the leading reporting framework for companies around the world. Originally founded by Ceres and the Tellus Institute in 1997, GRI is now headquartered in the Netherlands and is recognized for collaborating with UNEP. GRI operates as an independent, nonprofit organization and seeks input from over three thousand experts in business, labor, and civil sectors for contributions to their guidelines (www.globalreporting.org).

Version 3.1 of the guidelines (referred to as *G3.1*) was published in 2011 and is divided into two parts. Part 1 describes how to report. Part 2 describes what to report, including its list of performance indicators, which are organized into the three categories of economic, environmental, and social. According to GRI, "indicator protocols" are like the recipe behind the performance indicators. These protocols provide guidance concerning key terms from the indicator, compiling methodologies, relevance and intended scope of the indicator, in addition to technical information (GRI, 2012).

Part 1, "Reporting Principles and Guidance," includes the following (GRI, 2012):

- Principles to define report content: materiality, stakeholder inclusiveness, sustainability context, and completeness
- Principles to define report quality: balance, comparability, accuracy, timeliness, reliability, and clarity
- Guidance on how to set the report boundary

Materiality of information is a very important concern for sustainability reporting. Determining what is material involves working with stakeholders to better understand what they want to see. This is not a one-way decision made by the company. As mentioned in the metrics chapter, materiality should be defined both from the inside out and from the outside in.

Part 2 of the GRI guidance includes the following standard disclosures (GRI, 2000-2011, p. 19):

- Strategy and profile: disclosures that set the overall context for understanding organizational performance such as its strategy, profile, and governance
- Management approach: disclosures that cover how an organization addresses a given set of topics in order to provide context for understanding performance in a specific area
- Performance indicators: indicators that elicit comparable information on the economic, environmental, and social performance of the organization

As with a company's SMS, planning is an important part of putting together a successful sustainability report. The end result is not just a compilation of data points pulled from various initiatives around the corporation. Starting with key company strategies, it's necessary to find the data to support progress made (or the lack thereof) on those strategies and to report them with a sense of perspective that will satisfy the intended reader. Stakeholder feedback on report drafts can help to ensure that the right information is included and that it is explained in a clear and transparent manner. Are there any gaps in the data? Have goals been adjusted from year to year based upon performance? Are there any important trends to recognize?

Thinking about who will be reading the report can also help to ensure its clarity and value. As noted above, readers include a mix of potential customers, investors, business partners, and employees. Finding clear messages to relate to each and all of these groups can be a challenge, but linking the strategies and goals with the metrics can help to facilitate communication. Using graphs and tables can be very helpful, as long as they are not overly complicated. Benchmarking the results internally among divisions or externally against competitors can be useful as well.

One Report and Integrated Reporting

As sustainability reporting continues to become more common for companies, the move to combining sustainability reporting and financial information into one overarching report is becoming more common as well. As this trend continues, more and more CFOs have become involved with sustainability reporting as CEOs have somewhat stepped to the side.

This move is partially a byproduct of the need for better quality data. As companies move into the field of sustainability reporting, they often find that the data they need is not necessarily at their fingertips. Tracking systems and analyses often require upgrades in order to make certain that the numbers presented are correct and can be corroborated. Involving the finance department can help to make those numbers materialize and the surrounding processes smoother.

Further, investors are beginning to look at sustainability reports more and more. The finance department can help to ensure that the right types of data are included in the overall, unified report. Often, accounting firms are engaged to offer assurance for at least parts of the data—the most material of indicators presented (Mehallow, 2012).

Companies have also begun to make their reports a two-way form of communication. The printed or PDF copy is still available, but often an online version is made available, providing the opportunity for stakeholders to add comments. Videos and additional data links further enrich the presentation and allow for a deeper dive for those who are interested.

For now, integrated reporting is only being accomplished by a handful of companies such as Novo Nordisk, Philips, and United Technologies Corporation. It takes careful planning and strategic thinking to accomplish this type of reporting, but as companies begin to improve their focus on what is truly material and how their sustainability performance metrics relate to the future of their business, this kind of reporting can create real value.

The goal of integrated reporting is to show how company leaders are thinking strategically about sustainability and contextualizing that information across the business. These reports should explain their long-term vision regarding their environmental and social impacts as well as how their strategies and goals are working to improve those impacts to create a robust future for the company. This is more than a laundry list of initiatives or accomplishments. A successful report frames the sustainability objectives according to the company's vision and relates those objectives to the business value that they create. The information presented should include input from critical partners and stakeholders. It should also describe the resources and infrastructure devoted to the success of specified goals and targets (BSR, 2012).

The International Integrated Reporting Council (IIRC) is a global organization devoted to developing a framework to encourage integrated reporting. They are currently working with companies around the world to develop a pilot program. GRI is also in the process of revising its guidelines to promote integrated reporting. Version 4 is expected to be released in 2013 (BSR, 2012).

Concluding Thoughts

It is a very exciting time in the field of sustainability reporting. With such a high number of companies preparing sustainability reports at a minimum, and with upward of 75 percent of those companies using the GRI framework, this is good news for the field. Challenges remain as many companies have just begun to dip their toes in the area of reporting, only to find out how much they have to learn (Mehallow, 2012).

Many more changes should be expected over the next decade and even in the next half-dozen years. Will GRI continue to lead the way? Will IIRC become the new darling? Or will another upstart steal the spotlight? Bloomberg L.P. made news in the fall of 2012 when it backed the Sustainability Accounting Standards Board's intent to create a new set of standards to better quantify nonfinancial information (Environmental Leader, 2012).

Whatever standard or framework takes the lead, it is encouraging to know that companies around the globe are realizing that sustainability is here to stay and that it offers real business value. Those companies pursuing shared value through their supply chains are investing in communities that will pay it back to them. Reporting on these endeavors in a coherent and connected way will help to ensure their viability and continued success.

Supplementary Reading Suggestions

The following white paper produced by the Center for Corporate Citizenship at Boston College is highly recommended for providing an overall perspective on sustainability reporting, including information regarding the major players in the field:

> Boston College Center for Corporate Citizenship (Boston College). (2010). How to read a corporate social responsibility report. Boston: Boston College Center for Corporate Citizenship. Available for free download from:
> http://www.bcccc.net/index.cfm?pageId=2053&printview=true

SustainAbility's series of surveys on sustainability reporting always make for interesting reading. Their most recent report is available as follows:

> SustainAbility. (2010). Reporting change; reader's and reporters survey 2010. Futerra Sustainability Communications Ltd, SustainAbility Ltd and KPMG International Cooperative. Available for free download from:
> http://www.sustainability.com/library/reporting-change.

Referenced below is a solid, practical guide for reporting aimed toward small and medium enterprises or SMEs. The guide is straightforward and includes some case studies for illustration:

> Tng, W. (2010). *Sustainability reporting and SMEs: a closer look at the GRI.* Strategic Sustainability. Available for free download from:
> http://www.sustainabilityconsulting.com/extra-resources/sustainability-reporting-and-smes-a-closer-look-at-the-gri.html.

To review the award-winning sustainability reports mentioned in this chapter, refer to the following links:

> Coca-Cola Enterprises 2010-2011 report: http://www.thecoca-colacompany.com/citizenship/reporting.html

> Nike 2007-2009 report:
> http://www.nikebiz.com/crreport/pdf/?language=en-US

References

Boston College Center for Corporate Citizenship (Boston College). (2010). *How to read a corporate social responsibility report.* Boston: Boston College Center for Corporate Citizenship.

BSR. (2012). Reporting on sustainability strategy. *BSR insight.* Retrieved from: https://www.bsr.org/en/our-insights/bsr-insight-article/reporting-on-sustainability-strategy

Ceres. (2011). Nike wins top Ceres-ACCA award for best sustainability reporting. Retrieved from: http://www.ceres.org/press/press-releases/nike-wins-top-ceres-acca-award-for-best-sustainability-reporting

The Coca-Cola Company (Coca-Cola). (2011). Reasons to believe, 2010-2011 sustainability report. Retrieved from: http://www.thecoca-colacompany.com/citizenship/reporting.html

CorporateRegister.com. (2012). The CR reporting awards 2012. Retrieved from: http://www.corporateregister.com/crra/

Environmental Leader. (2012). Bloomberg-backed group to set sustainability standards. Retrieved from: http://www.environmentalleader.com/2012/10/09/bloomberg-backed-group-to-set-sustainability-standards/

Ernst & Young. (2011). Leading corporate sustainability issues in the 2012 proxy season: is your board prepared? Ernst & Young. Retrieved from: http://www.ey.com/Publication/vwLUAssets/2012_proxy_season/$FILE/2012_proxy_season.pdf

Global Reporting Initiative (GRI). (2000-2011). *RG, sustainability reporting guidelines, version 3.1.* Amsterdam: Global Reporting Initiative.

Global Reporting Initiative (GRI). (2012). G 3.1 guidelines; G 3.1 overview. Retrieved Nov. 10, 2012 from:

https://www.globalreporting.org/reporting/latest-guidelines/g3-1-guidelines/Pages/default.aspx

KPMG. (2011). *KPMG international survey of corporate responsibility reporting 2011*. Retrieved from: http://www.kpmg.com/global/en/issuesandinsights/articlespublicati ons/corporate-responsibility/pages/2011-survey.aspx

Mehallow, C. (2012). Where sustainability reporting is headed: an E&Y and GreenBiz survey. Retrieved from: http://www.triplepundit.com/2012/01/sustainability-reporting-headed-preview-ey-greenbiz-survey/

Nike, Inc. (n.d.) Goals and principles index. Retrieved from: http://www.nikebiz.com/crreport/content/about/1-4-8-guidelines-and-principles-index.php?cat=governance-accountability

Nike, Inc. (2010). Corporate responsibility report FY07-09. Retrieved from: http://www.nikebiz.com/crreport/pdf/?language=en-US

Palenberg, M. A., Reinicke, W. H., & Witte, J. M. (2009). Trends in non-financial reporting. Global Public Policy Institute.

Peavler, R. (2012). The Sarbanes-Oxley Act and the Enron scandal - why are they important? Retrieved from: http://bizfinance.about.com/od/smallbusinessfinancefaqs/a/sarbanes -oxley-act-and-enron-scandal.htm

Tng, W. (2010). *Sustainability reporting and SMEs: a closer look at the GRI*. Strategic Sustainability. Retrieved from: http://www.sustainabilityconsulting.com/extra-resources/sustainability-reporting-and-smes-a-closer-look-at-the-gri.html

Chapter 15

Design, Marketing, and Stewardship

Never tell people how to do things. Tell them what to do and they will surprise you with their ingenuity.

—General George S. Patton, Jr.

Introduction

Part of sustainability management means believing in the people who make up your organization. Beginning with the vision and mission and continuing throughout the organization, the sign of an excellent company is evidenced by the people involved.

Designing for sustainability fits within these parameters. We may take design for granted, but every product and service you use today was designed in some manner. In the best cases, careful planning goes into the production of a product or service.

A backward example is to think about how airports have been redesigned to accommodate increased security procedures following the September 11, 2001, attacks on the World Trade Center. Many airports are still revising their security check-in areas to handle the increase in space required. It has taken years to streamline the process. This is a real-life example of how *not* to design a process.

Past: Design for Production Efficiency

The design of most products involves several steps, beginning with product planning, conceptual design, and detailed design before it goes into the manufacturing stage. Researchers have found that roughly 75 percent of the cost of a product is committed by the end of the conceptual design stage (Sousa, 2008). This means that it is very difficult to reduce costs or to change the impacts of a product after this phase.

Planning ahead has therefore become very important in product design. Coupling the design process with the engineering of product assembly has helped many companies to reduce the ultimate cost of the product. Designing for easy parts fabrication, assembly, repair, and service can have a big impact on the quality of the product as well as its ultimate success.

The *Rule of 10* is a concept in manufacturing that stipulates that it costs ten times as much to repair or fix a problem at each progressive stage of its assembly. So, if a part has already been produced, it costs ten times as much to fix the problem. If it has already been assembled, it multiplies the problem by another ten times and so on, as shown below (Anderson, 2012):

The Rule of 10

Level of Completion	Cost to Find and Repair Defect
the part itself	X
at sub-assembly	10X
at final assembly	100X
at the dealer/distributor	1,000X
at the customer	10,000X

Careful planning in the design process can avoid these costly mistakes and can help to make the manufacturing process more efficient.

Present: Design for Efficiency and Environment

From a different perspective, the Rule of 10 can be applied to saving energy used by a product. Amory Lovins has written and spoken many times about the multiples of energy saved by designing products that use less energy. For example, since so much efficiency is lost in the production and distribution of electricity from a traditional coal-fired power plant, saving just a kilowatt of energy (a "negawatt") at the consumption end can save as much as ten times the energy needed at the production end. Figure 15.1 below illustrates this concept.

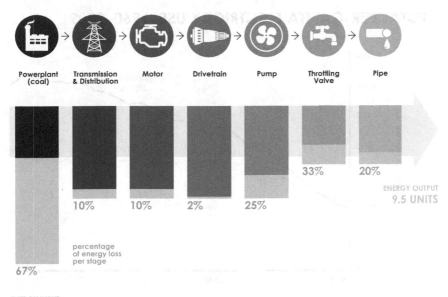

Figure 15.1: Energy Savings Multiplier Effect
(Lovins, 2007)

By increasing the efficiency of consumer appliances, for example, the energy needed at the power plant is reduced by up to a power of ten. California has been a leader in this area, spearheading efficiencies in refrigeration and other consumer appliances. The growth of energy use in California versus the rest of the United States has been much slower, in spite of the fact that California's population has doubled since 1970 while the US population grew by roughly 40 percent in that same period. Figure 15.2 below shows a comparison of electricity use in California versus the rest of the United States.

TOTAL PER-CAPITA ELECTRICITY USE, 1960–2009

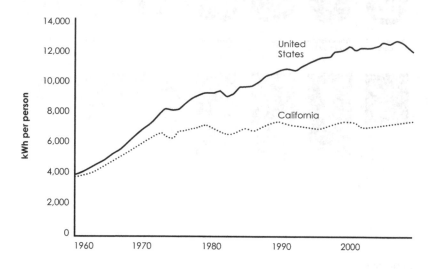

Rocky Mountain Institute ©2011. For more information see www.RMI.org/ReinventingFire.

Figure 15.2: Per Capita Electricity of California versus the United States
(RMI, 1990-2012)

This analysis can be applied to environmental stewardship overall as well. Emphasis on pollution prevention or P2 is growing in the sustainability field. Under the Pollution Prevention Act of 1990, the EPA has established pollution prevention initiatives and programs for various industries. Designing products that use fewer resources and cause less pollution are preferable and can reduce the overall cost of production (EPA, 2011).

In addition, the EPA initiated a Design for the Environment program that partners with businesses, NGOs, and academia to reduce toxic chemicals in products. Design for the Environment's product labeling and certification informs consumers as to whether or not a particular product meets EPA safety requirements. The organization also provides best practices in areas from auto refinishing to nail salons (http://www.epa.gov/dfe). Whether this program goes far enough is a source of continuing debate, but it does provide a level of supervision that promotes dialogue in the industry.

Integrated Design

Using integrated design can help a company to see beyond the cost barriers when making design improvements that can ultimately lead to dramatic cost and energy reductions. By spending more in one area, it may reduce costs in another. For example, architects and builders traditionally speak of the diminishing benefits of investing in higher insulation for the building envelope and windows. Yet if a building is super-insulated and is properly engineered for heating, cooling, and lighting (including daylight, task lighting, and individualized temperature controls), significant savings can be produced as a result of the systems required for the building itself.

This concept is called "tunneling through the cost barrier" (Lovins, 2010) and it was used recently in the retrofit of the Empire State Building. A collaborative project between the building's owner, Jones Lang LaSalle, Johnson Controls, the Clinton Climate Initiative, and RMI, the building underwent a "deep retrofit" producing energy savings of 38 percent or $4.4 million per year with a payback period of three years. By rebuilding and replacing the existing windows on site and converting them to very efficient windows, as well as increasing insulation and reducing heat load on the building, the project avoided having to replace the building's chillers, a savings of $14 million overall (RMI, 2009).

The LEED certification program sponsored by the US Green Building Council provides for a similar approach to holistic design. The various parties involved in the building design are encouraged to meet early in the design process to find integrated solutions to design challenges. The point system for LEED has undergone various improvements including improved air quality and other social benefits beyond just energy savings and resource use.

But a true collaboration encourages creative thinking across barriers. This type of engagement leads to the creation of new ideas, ideas that extend beyond the normal solutions. Putting designers in the same room with other stakeholders involved—engineers, manufacturers, customers, managers, and even regulators—can create the type of atmosphere that truly breaks the mold of traditional design and leads to the discovery of new ways to resolve design problems. The result can be that it may actually cost less to save more.

Life Cycle Analysis

Using LCA can be a very effective means to improve design at the earliest stages and to improve overall cost and environmental effects. At the same time, it can be difficult to conduct a detailed LCA of a product before the design is relatively complete. And even then, a complete LCA can be extremely costly. Some companies simply aren't interested in committing the necessary resources.

This practice is changing, however, with the development of sophisticated software programs and cloud computing, which can be used to estimate LCAs of products based on preliminary specifications and presumed material use. Having this information available early in the design stage can have an enormous impact on the environmental effects of a product. This information can also help manufacturers and service providers understand how to make changes in the design of their products or services early in the game, thereby increasing profitability and addressing the impacts that their business has on the environment and society (Sousa, 2008).

Figure 15.3 below shows the connection between design and manufacturing costs. As you can see, 75 percent of the cost is committed early in the design process, even before the manufacturing process has begun.

Design Effect in Manufacturing Cost

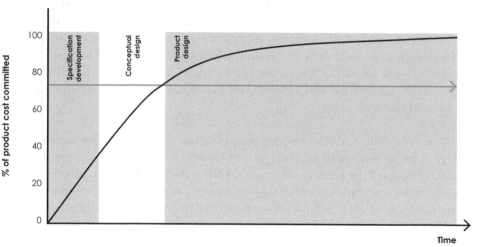

Figure 15.3: Connection between Design and Manufacturing Cost
(Sousa, 2008)

Today, as companies are becoming more aware of their supply chain (or value chain), many are using LCA to address the sustainable consumption of their products and services. For some companies, the greatest resource use can occur after the product is sold to consumers. Computers and cell phones are one example. Clothing is another. Levi Strauss has been developing ways to "stonewash" its jeans with just stones and no water. It has also begun marketing its lower water use to consumers, encouraging them to wash the jeans less or not at all. Recommendations have even been made to put the jeans in the freezer to kill odors and germs rather than washing them (Kaufman, 2011).

This reduces resource consumption, reduces pollution, and improves the value chains for the larger companies who work with smaller producers in developing countries. With markets for goods growing rapidly as developing countries grow, multinational companies see this as a powerful market opportunity for growth (UNEP, 2006).

Future: Design for Sustainability

Companies today are beginning to understand the larger impacts of globalization and growth as well as the constraints of limited resources. The risks to their supply chain for necessary resources are pushing product design to account for these risks. Examples abound. Nestlé is engaging with farmers in developing countries to improve their agricultural practices and to ensure an available supply of the products they need. Nike is working to eliminate toxic chemicals from its supply chain. Coca-Cola and PepsiCo are working to reduce the water intensity of their production processes as well as to improve water resources in developing countries.

Beyond the environmental concerns, many companies are now including social issues in their design considerations. Population growth has largely been ignored (or avoided) by environmentalists over the past decades, but in recent years, they have started to engage in more forward-thinking discussions concerning these issues. Environmental conferences have begun to add sessions on world population growth and its impact upon the world's ecosystems as well as overall human health. The stress of population pressure in developing countries is now recognized as both a risk and an opportunity for corporations and product design.

Women's health, as another example, is starting to be considered a sustainability issue. Though it may not be an obvious design issue in the sense of LCA or the design of products or services, the design involved with how a company manufactures products and how that company treats its labor force really is a design issue, is it not? Offering fertility planning education and contraceptives to women in developing countries has been found to reduce the rate of population growth. Allowing women to plan their pregnancies provides for better overall family health, better education opportunities for both women and children, and a higher quality of life overall. Besides these benefits to the local society, companies benefit by having a more productive work force with fewer unplanned pregnancies and fewer women unexpectedly dropping out of the work force.

BSR, a nonprofit organization focused on sustainability, initiated a program in 2007 in collaboration with a number of corporations and other NGOs to provide women's health education in developing countries around the world. Dubbed the HERproject (Health Enables Returns), it was implemented in roughly fifty factories in 2012 with the goal to expand to many more factories around the globe. The program is sponsored by local factories and facilitated by local nonprofits and uses picture-based educational brochures that can be customized for each country, eliminating literacy or translation concerns.

The HERproject pilot programs have been found to produce up to a four to one payback for the educational program investments made by companies supporting these efforts. Companies that participate include the garment industry, agriculture, as well as the communications and technology industries. BSR uses its network to connect these companies with local NGOs to facilitate health care delivery, financial support, and worker training to low-income women employed by the companies (BSR, 2012).

Design for future sustainability therefore includes social issues as well as environmental issues. Energy conservation and concerns about climate change will certainly be prominent, but the connections between the environmental impacts and social impacts are becoming increasingly apparent. Sustainability reporting and the movement toward one report may be a contributor to this trend. What gets measured gets managed. The connections that are reported begin to be managed as well, to the benefit of corporate productivity as well as social and environmental welfare.

Marketing for Sustainability

Companies around the world are searching for that sweet spot with respect to marketing their sustainability claims without overreaching and being accused of greenwashing. Consumers are interested in purchasing sustainable products with some price sensitivity, but they can also be skeptical of a company's claims regarding product sustainability. Various seals of approval—from LEED certification to the EPA's Design for the Environment program—are available, but as of yet there is no universal certification program for the sustainability of products.

The Energy Star rating program has been very successful with respect to consumers, but it covers only certain consumer products and has only recently been expanded to include electronics, a growing source of energy use worldwide. Companies use the ISO standards and the GRI reporting system to certify and rate other companies in their own supply chain, but most consumers are not familiar with these certifications.

A recent global survey found that people in developing countries are significantly more interested in their own sustainability behavior as well as the sustainability of the products that they purchase over those in developed countries. A survey of over six thousand consumers in six countries across the world conducted by SustainAbility and GlobeScan in 2012 had some surprising results. They found that 51 percent of consumers in the developing markets of Brazil, China, and India reported purchasing products for environmental and social benefits, versus just 22 percent of consumers in Germany, the United Kingdom, and the United States. Consumers in developing countries were also more than twice as likely to say that they would pay more for sustainable products—60 percent as opposed to 26 percent in developed countries (Enviro Leader, 2012).

At the same time, the survey showed that consumers remained skeptical about product claims and that they are relatively uneducated with respect to determining the sustainability of a particular product. Although many said that they wished to purchase sustainably produced goods, a large majority of the entire survey pool (63 percent) reported that they were not aware of how or where to find that kind of information (Enviro Leader, 2012). This is indeed a challenge for the marketing efforts of companies who are taking sustainability seriously.

Besides the opportunity to market sustainably produced goods in developing countries, there are other marketing opportunities available to companies seeking to expand their markets. Referred to as "the bottom of the pyramid," such markets offer great opportunity, but they can also require employment of a different marketing model.

Unilever has created a successful program model using local women in India who are trained in health, nutrition, and hygiene. Armed with Unilever products, these women learn communication skills in seminars and spread their information through software customized for illiterate users. These women also train Unilever managers and sales people. The program has grown from fifty villages in 2000 to over eighty thousand villages in 2007 all over India. Entitled the Shakti Amma (meaning empowered mother) program, it has earned Unilever over $250 million in areas that would otherwise be unreachable using ordinary business models (Googins, Mirvis & Rochlin, 2007, p. 181).

HP has also used unconventional marketing techniques to promote its products in Africa. It created an early infant diagnosis program in Kenya, developing databases and information-transfer systems using mobile phones. This improved the speed of diagnosis and encouraged treatment of infants in areas that were normally difficult to reach. The program has established HP as a reliable and responsible business partner for the government of Kenya and for other governments in the area. The program has led to a growth in commercial opportunities for HP well beyond its social investment in the diagnosis program (BSR, 2011).

Marketing at the bottom of the pyramid as presented in these examples can also apply in developed countries as well. Even cities such as Washington, DC, include neighborhoods where people may go unnoticed by census reports or business marketing strategies. Social Compact, an NGO that collects market information for inner cities, has reported that the Columbia Heights neighborhood of Washington, DC, is much denser and is growing faster than US Census reports suggest. In fact, they found the population to be 51 percent higher due to a large influx of immigrants functioning on a largely cash economy. Companies using this information can capture the demand from these otherwise unrecognized markets (Googins, Mirvis & Rochlin, 2007, pp. 181-182).

Concluding Thoughts

As you can see, design can encompass more than just product life cycles. Marketing can incorporate more than advertising through conventional channels. Today's leading companies are looking beyond the traditional models to include social structures that are organized differently than those in the developed world. Using local channels and harnessing local creativity can provide significant opportunities for growth in markets as well as opportunities to reduce pollution and the quantity of resources needed.

There are indeed many challenges associated with resource depletion, climate change, and population growth, but trusting the creativity of local communities can lead to real progress. As General Patton advised, don't tell them how to do it; tell them what you need and let them have at it.

Supplementary Reading Suggestions

RMI and Amory Lovins have published an excellent peer-reviewed book, *Reinventing Fire: Bold Business Solutions for the New Energy Era*. This analysis contains integrated solutions to resolve the energy needs of the United States by 2050 with no oil, coal, or nuclear energy, and one-third less natural gas. No new inventions or policy changes are needed; rather, market-based solutions are described that stretch across various industries to conserve energy and promote renewable energy resources. It received the 2011 Book of the Year award from ForeWord Reviews as well as many other accolades.

> Lovins, A.B. & Rocky Mountain Institute. (2011). *Reinventing fire: bold business solutions for the new energy era*. White River Junction, VT: Chelsea Green.

To learn more about the Empire State Building retrofit, visit the Empire State Building website to download various white papers, presentations, and videos of the players involved:
http://www.esbnyc.com/sustainability_energy_efficiency.asp.

You can also read a summary of the Empire State Building project on RMI's website, which also includes links to more information about this and other deep retrofit projects:

http://blog.rmi.org/blog_empire_state_retrofit_surpasses_ener gy_savings_expectations#savings.

The UNEP *Design for Sustainability* document referenced in this chapter is an excellent source of information and includes many case studies and practical tools, including common sense recommendations for sustainable design and tools for creative group exercises, including brainwriting and mind mapping.

United Nations Environment Programme (UNEP). (2006). *Design for sustainability: a practical approach for developing economies.* Available for free download at: http://www.unep.fr/scp/publications/details.asp?id=DTI/082 6/PA.

References

Anderson, D.M. (2012). Design for manufacturability. Retrieved from: http://www.design4manufacturability.com/DFM_article.htm

BSR. (2011). Emerging markets: where sustainability is simply good business. Retrieved from: http://www.bsr.org/en/bsr-conference/session-summary-view/2011/emerging-markets-where-sustainability-is-simply-good-business

BSR. (2012). Beyond incrementalism with Justin Adams: accelerating solutions in the food, energy, and water nexus. Retrieved from: http://2012-ny.bsr.org/en/sessions/summaries-view/beyond-incrementalism-with-justin-adams-accelerating-solutions-in-the-food-

Environmental Leader (Enviro Leader). (2012). Sustainability a key factor for consumers, survey finds. Retrieved from: http://www.environmentalleader.com/2012/11/26/sustainability-a-key-factor-for-consumers-survey-finds/

EPA. (2011). Pollution prevention (P2). Retrieved from: http://www.epa.gov/p2/pubs/basic.htm

Googins, B., Mirvis, P, & Rochlin, S. (2007). *Beyond good company; next generation corporate citizenship.* New York: Palgrave MacMillan.

Kaufman, L. (2011) Stone-washed blue jeans (minus the washed). *The New York Times.* Retrieved from: http://www.nytimes.com/2011/11/02/science/earth/levi-strauss-tries-to-minimize-water-use.html?pagewanted=all

Lovins, A.B. (2007). Public lectures in advanced energy efficiency: 2. Industry. Retrieved from: http://www.rmi.org/Content/Files/E07-03_Stanford_2Industry.pdf

Lovins, A. B. (2010). Integrative design: a disruptive source of expanding returns to investments in energy efficiency. Retrieved from: http://www.rmi.org/Knowledge-Center/Library/2010-09_IntegrativeDesign

Rocky Mountain Institute (RMI). (1990-2012), Total per-capita electricity use, 1960-2009. Retrieved from: http://www.rmi.org/RFGraph-total_per_capita_eletricity_use

Rocky Mountain Institute (RMI). (2009). Empire State Building: putting a new
   face on an American icon. Retrieved from:
   http://www.rmi.org/Content/Files/GetInvolved_Toolkit_Empire%20
   State%20Building%20Retrofit.pdf
Sousa, I. (2008). Part 1: The genesis of Sustainable Minds - The conception of
   'learning surrogate LCA. Sustainable Minds. Retrieved from:
   http://www.sustainableminds.com/industry-blog/part-1-genesis-
   sustainable-minds-conception-learning-surrogate-lca
United Nations Environment Programme (UNEP). (2006). *Design for sustainability: a practical approach for developing economies.* Paris: United Nations
   Environment Programme Division of Technology, Industry, and Economics, Delft University of Technology.

Chapter 16

Innovation

If I had asked people what they wanted, they would have said "faster horses."

—*Henry Ford*

Introduction

One could argue that innovation has been part of business since business began—or then again, since the beginning of life itself. Birds, bees, and every other species have been innovators, finding ways to survive as the world's climate has changed over the past millennia. The world's species will certainly be challenged to find new solutions as human-induced climate change creates more rapid variations in the ecosystem.

Innovation has largely been attributed to entrepreneurs in the business world. Entrepreneurs embody the pinnacle of capitalist idealism: creating new products in the face of challenge and risk. However, entrepreneurs aren't necessarily risk takers, as they won't succeed if they take too many risks. Ultimately, both entrepreneurs and established businesses depend upon innovation (and perhaps a bit of risk) to create their space in the market.

What about the connection between innovation and sustainability? Does innovation drive sustainability or is it the other way around? As is typically the answer when sustainability questions arise, it depends.

Early in this book, when investigating the business case for sustainability in Chapter 3, we visited the survey results from MIT and Boston Consulting Group. Their surveys over the past several years repeatedly found that those companies who possess higher expertise in sustainability management are more confident about their ability to create overall value. On the other hand, when top management is less informed about the benefits of sustainability management, they are much more reluctant to pursue the benefits of environmental and social investments (MIT & BCG, 2009, 2011).

This is true for investment in sustainable-related innovation as well. Companies that are interested and more informed about innovations related to environmental and social impacts are much more likely to pursue those investments and will therefore reap the resulting rewards.

From Compliance to Paradigm Shifts

Timberland provides an excellent example of a company that has gone beyond regulation compliance to find business value in leading the market in environmental and social innovation. When searching for appropriate metrics and standards related to tanning leather in its supply chain, Timberland decided to develop its own. It then reached out to competitors in the industry to build a more robust framework.

Not satisfied with the metrics commonly available at the time (this was in the early 1990s before the GRI framework had been developed by Ceres), Timberland worked with its own suppliers and with others in the apparel industry including Nike. They put together their own index of indicators for environmental quality and worked with tanneries around the world to help them meet these new, higher standards. The result was not only better environmental performance but also a simplification in processes and oversight.

Now, Timberland is working toward expanding what it calls the Higg Index to other apparel companies. They have also developed a "nutritional label" for their products allowing customers to easily identify the carbon impact, chemicals used, and resources consumed in the production of a particular product (Blaisdell, 2012).

As companies like Timberland continue to find value in their supply chains through improving sustainability, they arc becoming more and more aware of how to communicate these improvements to their various stakeholders. For example, Timberland has moved to quarterly, online sustainability reporting. This allows for more timely updates and opens the door to feedback from the community. Transparency is seen as an opportunity, not a risk. By being straightforward about their challenges as well as their achievements, Timberland is less likely to be charged with greenwashing and more likely to receive objective feedback from their stakeholder groups.

The shift from merely compliance to adopting new business models is the paradigm shift seen among leading businesses today. Companies that embrace sustainability and view it as an opportunity for innovation can stay ahead of the regulatory curve, maintaining an advantage over competitors.

HP used a similar approach in Europe when it learned in 2002 that it would be required to recycle waste from its products in proportion to sales. It quickly teamed up with three other companies to form a recycling program that was much more efficient than that of its competitors due to the program's scale and cooperative efforts. In addition to saving over $100 million over a four-year period, HP also enhanced its reputation with regulators given its proactive stance.

HP's positive reputation paid off in 2006 when Europe began to consider regulations prohibiting the use of hexavalent chromium, used to prevent corrosion in products, which had been linked to cancer. In part due to its positive reputation, HP was able to convince authorities to postpone the regulation for one year, providing the company with time to develop alternatives in a more cost-effective manner (Nidumolu, Prahalad, & Rangaswami, 2009).

Sometimes adoption of the new paradigm means rethinking your business model altogether. FedEx did so in 2004 when it acquired the Kinko's copy chain. This purchase allowed FedEx to enter the document delivery business in a new way. Rather than shipping printed copies of documents across the country, it could receive a customer's document in electronic form. The document could then be printed in the destination city and shipped via a short truck ride rather than via airplane through its main Tennessee hub. FedEx saved on transportation costs and the customer gained production time through a reduction in delivery time (Nidumolu, Prahalad, & Rangaswami, 2009).

Another example of rethinking business platforms is the electric grid. Companies like Cisco Systems, HP, and Dell are working with utilities companies Duke Energy and Florida Power & Light Company to develop a "smart" grid. This new approach to energy management will employ digital technology and energy storage from various sources, including consumers with electric cars, to manage power generation and transmission. This approach will make it possible for renewable energy resources to enter the market in larger quantities, reducing our need for coal-fired power plants and other fossil fuel-generated power (Nidumolu, Prahalad, & Rangaswami, 2009).

Business Value

In a survey conducted in 2004 by Arthur D. Little, out of forty technology companies across the United States and Europe, 95 percent of businesses stated that sustainability–driven innovation has the potential to deliver business value. Almost one quarter stated that it definitely provided business value. But there are still barriers to overcome. Fully integrating sustainability into product design and strategy remains a challenge. A growing number of companies have begun to focus, however, on market growth as opposed to risk management (Keeble, et al, 2005, p. 3).

Sony is a company that is driving sustainability into its product design and supply chain through its management systems. In 2005, Sony set long-term goals and mid-term targets for each division. These targets included reducing the number of parts, increasing the recycled content, and reducing the overall weight of its products. Each division receives guidance and education from the corporate headquarters while award programs help to enhance interest and individual employee participation. Using LCAs has helped Sony to identify where resource and energy reductions can be made and priorities set. Labeling products has helped to inform consumers about the company's progress (Keeble, et al, 2005, p. 13).

One example of social innovation comes from the expansion of micro-credits in developing countries. BanGente is one such commercial operation, offering microcredit loans to people in Venezuela. The UN has estimated that there are over ten million microbusinesses across Latin America employing over half of the working populace. Yet only 15 percent use commercial banks and less than 5 percent have access to financial products. The rest are forced to use informal financial markets, which charge very high interest rates. BanGente recognized this to be a growth opportunity.

The microcredits offered by BanGente and similar companies provide small loans to family businesses with only a few employees. Paperwork is minimal and decisions about credit worthiness are made on site, where advice is offered by employees trained in the local area. Most of these families have little education and yet the loan payback rate is 99 percent. Most of the money loaned is reinvested in the business or is used to pay for education expenses, home improvement, or health insurance (Keeble, et al, 2005, pp. 14-15).

Many microcredit loans go to women. Similarly, companies are finding that investing in women beyond issuing microcredits is smart business. Coca-Cola, for example, has created a sixteen-member Women's Leadership Council to recruit and support women in leadership positions at the company at all levels of its value chain. This includes farmers, distributors, suppliers, retailers, and recyclers. Their goal is to provide economic empowerment to five million women by 2020 through loans, training, and network support.

Like other companies and research institutions, Coca-Cola has found that women are much more likely to reinvest their earnings into their families and communities. They also tend to make the majority of the purchasing decisions for their households. "We know that women, as future consumers, account for $20 trillion of consumer expenditure. People talk about the emerging economies of China or India. Women, as a market opportunity, represent more [opportunity] than China, India, and the United States combined," said Charlotte Oades, global director of Coca-Cola's Women Empowerment Program. By rolling out pilot programs in India, Brazil, and the Philippines, Coca-Cola hopes to develop the program more fully and to expand it to its entire supply chain (BSR, 2012).

Innovation through Disruption

For established companies, innovation can sometimes be difficult to achieve on a continuing basis. Many concerns must be managed and it can seem overwhelming to take on new ideas when the old problems keep rearing their ugly heads. In addition, companies work hard to develop strategies and plans to succeed according to their current business model. Making a change in the middle of executing those strategies can seem like a threat to achieving the goals they worked so hard to create.

But disruption can also be a way to knock things loose—at least to a certain extent. Disruption can arise in various forms including technology changes, market globalization, new business models, consolidation or new players in the industry, or regulatory and political changes. These changes can be seen as risks or opportunities depending on how a business chooses to approach the situation.

In a survey of 750 leading companies conducted by IBM in 2006, over 50 percent of CEOs said that innovation in their industry resulted mostly from changes in the business environment. Only 20 percent of those surveyed said that innovation came from within their companies. These CEOs also said that they were planning significant changes over the next two years while only 15 percent said they had been "very successful" in managing change in the past. So, disruption happens, causing innovation whether a company likes it or not. And some CEOs are handling that disruption better than others (Applegate, 2007).

Role of Sustainability Management Systems

An SMS can provide the type of oversight needed to get the best results from innovation. The types of cross-functional communication and forward planning established by an SMS will help to ensure that innovations are implemented properly across the company and that any unforeseen negative impacts are more likely to be recognized and mitigated.

Are there stakeholders impacted by the change? Are products up or down the supply chain affected? Does the new product mean that other areas of the business may become obsolete? When Apple introduced the iPhone and the iPad, for example, did they fully understand how it would impact their laptop sales? It may have not been possible to fully understand the effects early on, but having a robust SMS in place would facilitate that type of investigation.

Some companies create separate divisions or venture groups to manage innovation and disruptive change. This may provide those groups with free reign, helping to reduce the risk of loss due to an unsuccessful venture. Other businesses, in contrast, keep innovation development under close supervision and in close contact, allowing for the integration of ideas into the overall business strategies and plans. Both approaches can work, but using a management system to oversee the entire process helps to promote and ensure both collaboration and engagement with important stakeholders.

Concluding Thoughts

> *Your paradigm is so intrinsic to your mental process that you are hardly aware of its existence until you try to communicate with someone with a different paradigm.*
>
> —*Donella Meadows*

Dana Meadows remains an icon for innovation in the sustainability field. Her paper, "Leverage Points: Places to Intervene in a System," is one that anyone interested in sustainability should read. People often look for a magic bullet to resolve their problems, but as Dana points out, it can take a series of steps and programs to find a solution. Doing so requires teamwork and cooperation, communication and clear goals. It may also necessitate a paradigm shift in one's overall thinking; this can sometimes require a disruptive circumstance or series of circumstances (Meadows, 2009).

Similarly, Amory Lovins refers to "acupuncture points" to help an organization make a shift in its paradigms. A company must determine where its business processes or procedures are blocked. Stimulating new ideas or communication processes can help to clear those blockages. Innovation can then flow more freely through the system, enabling new paradigms and business models to emerge (Lovins, 2010).

Sustainability-driven innovation can provide the leverage or the acupuncture needed to move a business away from its stuck paradigms into a more responsible, efficient, and profitable future. Using an SMS can help to drive that innovation forward and to ensure that adequate resources are devoted to new ideas and products, and that the right teams of people are assigned to manage them.

Supplementary Reading Suggestions

BSR has conducted some very interesting sustainability conferences over the past several years and their website contains summaries of all sessions: http://2012-ny.bsr.org/.

The Dana Meadows article mentioned in this chapter is available for free download at: http://www.thesolutionsjournal.com/node/419.

The *Harvard Business Review* article below is highly recommended for a deeper dive into how sustainability can be a driver for innovation as well as recommended steps to follow in that process:

Nidumolu, R., Prahalad, C.K., Rangaswami, M.R. (2009). Why Sustainability Is Now the Key Driver of Innovation. Harvard Business Review. Retrieved from:

http://hbr.org/2009/09/why-sustainability-is-now-the-key-driver-of-innovation/es.

References

Applegate, L. M. (2007). Jumpstarting innovation: using disruption to your advantage. Harvard Business School. Retrieved from: http://hbswk.hbs.edu/item/5636.html

BSR. (2012). Investing in women is smart business. BSR Session Summary. Retrieved from: http://2012-ny.bsr.org/en/sessions/summaries-view/investing-in-women-is-smart-business

Blaisdell, B. & Kruschwitz, N. (2012) New ways to engage employees, suppliers and competitors in CSR. Retrieved from: http://sloanreview.mit.edu/feature/new-ways-to-engage-employees-suppliers-and-competitors-in-csr/

Keeble, J., Lyon, D., Vasallo, D., Hedstrom, G., & Sanchez, H. (2005). How leading companies are using sustainability-driven innovation to win tomorrow's customers. Arthur D. Little & Hedstrom Associates. Retrieved from: http://www.adlittle.com/reports.html?view=13

Lovins, A. B. (2010). Freeing America from its addiction to oil. CNN. Retrieved from: http://www.cnn.com/2010/OPINION/01/04/lovins.weaning.us.off.oil/index.html

Meadows, D. (2009). Leverage points: places to intervene in a system. Solutions (1)1, 41-49. Retrieved from: http://www.thesolutionsjournal.com/node/419

MIT Sloan Management Review & The Boston Consulting Group (MIT & BCG). (2009). *The business of sustainability*. Cambridge, MA: Massachusetts Institute of Technology. Available from: http://sloanreview.mit.edu/special-report/

MIT Sloan Management Review and The Boston Consulting Group (MIT & BCG). (2011). *Sustainability: the 'embracers' seize advantage*. Cambridge, MA: Massachusetts Institute of Technology. Available from: http://sloanreview.mit.edu/special-report/

Nidumolu, R., Prahalad, C.K., Rangaswami, M.R. (2009). Why sustainability is now the key driver of innovation. Harvard Business Review. Retrieved from: http://hbr.org/2009/09/why-sustainability-is-now-the-key-driver-of-innovation/es

Chapter 17

Conclusion

Even if you're on the right track, you'll be run over if you just sit there.
—*Will Rogers*

Business leaders around the world understand the importance of many of the concepts described in this book. Sustainability concepts may or may not be recognized as part of a typical business model, but more and more, they are becoming the norm. As mentioned in Chapter 3 regarding the business case for sustainability, the series of surveys conducted by MIT and Boston College have shown that companies that are well informed about sustainability are more inclined to embrace its principles and to apply those principles across the board and throughout the company's value chain. Companies that choose to ignore these concepts will find themselves struggling in an increasingly transparent and resource-constrained world. The embracers of sustainability, on the other hand, will be better prepared to meet these challenges.

The goal of this book is to provide an overview of the materials and the tools that are available to sustainability leaders today. The hope is that now you understand the right questions to ask in order to evaluate the relative benefit of these tools and frameworks, and to thereafter be able to customize them to fit your organization or business. As new ideas emerge, you will also be able to review them with a critical eye to determine whether or not they are worthwhile for consideration.

As in any review, pay attention to the source of those new ideas. Where did they come from? What is the background of the organization or author presenting these tools? To what industry would it apply best? Are there any proven examples as to the success of these tools? Who is using them now and do they have similar business challenges? Can you use these tools to drive innovation, to improve your place in the market, or to improve your position regarding natural or human capital?

As this book goes to print, the new GRI *G4* guidelines are poised for release. Concern has been expressed by some analysts that, while the field has shown an improved emphasis on materiality of reporting, the new guidelines will be too complex and onerous for pursuit by some companies. Others disagree. They argue that GRI has made significant changes to improve transparency and materiality, and that companies who just want a slick public relations report will no longer be able to hide. Regardless, it is clear that corporate social responsibility reporting and even integrated reporting of financials and sustainability are becoming the new normal and that the GRI parameters have become the predominant tools used by sustainability professionals today.

For you, combining the GRI guidelines with other performance frameworks such as Baldridge Criteria, or other certification programs such as the various standards provided by ISO, may prove to uncover the sweet spot for your company. The goal should always be to find the right balance between the three areas of responsibility for sustainability, to engage with your stakeholders to be better informed about market pressures, and to open lines of communication throughout your company, engaging with all levels as well as the value chain.

It is of course up to you and the other members of your management team to make these decisions. Hopefully the information presented here will give you the confidence and the capability necessary to make informed decisions about your future direction. Moving forward is key. Standing still is not an option. Onward.

Supplementary Reading Suggestions

For those interested in learning more about the GRI guidelines, visit GRI's website: www.globalreporting.org. Training sessions on GRI implementation is offered by various consulting companies that are well versed in these frameworks. You might consider enrolling in one of these sessions to improve your knowledge in this area.

As mentioned in the introduction, but worth emphasizing here, there are two excellent books on the subject of sustainability that go into greater detail than the information provided here. These books are both recommended reading for the Corporate Sustainability Strategy class mentioned in the preface:

> Blackburn, W. (2007). *The sustainability handbook.* Washington, DC: Environmental Law Institute.

This book presents a comprehensive treatise on the subject, outlining in more detail many of the concepts covered here. In addition, the second half of the book is comprised of various appendices that include sample forms and tables to be used in practice, lists and explanations of various standards and their application, as well as other resources and organizations available to support and advise the sustainability professional. I highly recommend it.

> Googins, B., Mirvis, P, & Rochlin, S. (2007). *Beyond good company; next generation corporate citizenship.* New York: Palgrave MacMillan.

This book focuses more on the social responsibility aspect of sustainability and it therefore complements the Blackburn book well, which emphasizes environmental responsibility. The authors provide numerous examples of companies who have enhanced their performance and brand equity by improving their performance from the social equity level. It is an interesting read and also provides good support for the professional seeking to build a business case for social welfare in the company and throughout the supply chain.

Finally, I would recommend Ray Anderson's book listed below. Ray followed many of the concepts described here. He is open and frank about his experiences—both successes and failures—and with their implementation. It is also a wonderful audio book if that format suits you. Read by Ray in his charming southern drawl, you can hear his enthusiasm for bringing Interface to a leadership position in sustainability. Ray Anderson passed away in 2012. He will be sorely missed.

> Anderson, R.C. (2009). *Confessions of a radical industrialist: profits, people, purpose – doing business by respecting the earth.* New York: St. Martin's Press.

References

Dobkowski-Joy, A. (2012). Are GRI's next-gen guidelines too complex? Green-Biz.com. Retrieved from: http://www.greenbiz.com/blog/2012/10/02/are-gris-next-gen-guidelines-too-complex

Henriques, A. (2012). GRI G4: an end to PR perfection? Getting accountability to work. Retrieved from: http://www.henriques.info/?p=1219

Scholz, K.M. (2012). Materiality in CSR reporting: the importance of GRI's G4 guidelines. Thomson Reuters. Retrieved from: http://sustainability.thomsonreuters.com/2012/11/30/materiality-in-csr-reporting-the-importance-of-gris-g4-guidelines/

Index